FAITH BREEZES

Faith Breezes

Glimpsing God's Glory
in Everyday Life

SUE HOLBROOK

Published in the United States by:
RIVER BREEZE PUBLICATIONS
P. O. Box 2084
Vero Beach, FL 32961-2084
www.sueholbrook.net

Faith Breezes: Glimpsing God's Glory in Everyday Life
Text © 2015 by Sue Holbrook
Cover and interior photographs © 2015 by Judy Deeson
Cover texture @ 2015 Foxey Squirrel
Book design by cj Madigan | shoebox-stories.com

ISBN 978-0-692-42500-8

1. Florida – Memoir – 21st Century – Non-Fiction.
2. Faith – Non-Fiction. 3. Grandparents – Non-Fiction.
4. Children – Non-Fiction. 5. Grandchildren – Non-Fiction.
6. Family (Interpersonal relations) – Non-Fiction.
7. South – Non-Fiction.

To my husband, Ed
who has shared most of this life journey with me.
No girl ever had a better partner for this roller coaster called life.
I love and appreciate you more than you know.

And in memory of the Kennedy team—
My parents, Purnell and Nannie Lou, and
My aunt and uncle, Clyde and Tom—
In the imagery of Isaiah 51:1, they are
the rock from which I was cut, the quarry from which I was hewn.

CONTENTS

Foreword   ix
Introduction   xi
About the Book   xiii

 *Spring*

A Group of Greats   3
My Calling   8
Camel. Goat. Whatever.   13
A Direct Message   16
A Woman Named Clyde   19
Salty Service   23
One Great Trip   26
On Faith and Friendship   30
Grandmother's Faith   34
Old Age, Gray Hairs & Bearing Fruit   37
The "W" Word   41
Snowed in...in Alabama   44
A Shining Light   49
Under His Feet   53
A Moment of Tooth   56

Summer

Accepting the Adventure	63
The Gloaming	68
Security Question	71
New Accessories	75
Cheers, Tears & Clouds of Witness	78
Two Aged Quilts	82
One Light, Two LIghts, Many Lights	86
Training Wheels	88
Peace ·	91
The Mother of the Bride	94
Two-Song Tom	99
The Cross on the Water	103
Carved Coconut Heads	106
The Super Moon	110

Fall

Borrowed Clothes	117
Learning From Daddy	121
Porches and Rocking Chairs	124
Action Heroes	127
Point A to Point A	131
Train Up a Child	135
The Prodigal Daughter	139
Honoring the Family	143
Just Keep Walking	146
Put on the Grits!	150
Contrasts	155
Dancing the Sky	159
Thanksgiving	163
Pitchfork Theology	166

Winter

Feet   173

Through Andrew's Eyes   177

A Mother Who Worked   181

Sing to the Lord   185

The Last Look   190

Embarrassment   193

A Thin Place   197

Friends   201

On the Arm of His Chair   205

Impossible Feats of Motherhood   208

Knocking on the Door   211

When Christmas Comes to Our House   215

And All the Pretties Were Left   219

The Husband   222

Manger Meditations   227

Acknowledgments   231

About the Author   232

FOREWORD

I first became really aware of Sue Holbrook when she took the Disciple class I was leading at the First United Methodist Church in Vero Beach, Florida. Oh, I knew her as a faithful member of the Chancel Choir sitting up front every Sunday, but I really learned who she was in that Bible study class. This woman with a deep faith could ask the hard questions. She was searching, and as leader of the class, it was a challenge for me. She made me grow along with her. The whole class benefited from her search for God and how he would use her.

I thought she would make a great teacher and urged her to teach a Bible study class. But that was not to be. God had other plans for her.

Sue took the Lay Speaker Course. She would say, "But I am never going to speak from that pulpit!" You do not tell God, "Never." She has given the message several times in our church— from that pulpit. Every Thursday we have a Ladies Luncheon. Since we are a downtown church, the attendance may include women from the nearby businesses or courthouse on their lunch break. The Ladies are faithful to her because she presents a message based on scripture. She does a series of talks. No one wants to miss any of them. She uses humor, her family, God's family and always prayer.

Soon Sue started writing an Internet blog. She calls it Faith Breezes. Again you become addicted to her beautiful message, God's message, with all the ways He uses her. Everything sounds like she has no worries, but during all this time, she has been through breast cancer surgery and her grandchildren have had medical needs that cannot be cured in a couple of days or weeks. We all got to see her become a redhead, a blonde and finally, just bald. The love of God did not diminish one iota. Her positive attitude continues.

Sue has several books inside of her, but she really wanted to write this book. Here you will find the real Sue. Be prepared to laugh, to cry, to question yourself and to grow in your own faith.

Coyla Boob
Retired Educator

INTRODUCTION

As a native of warm and sunny (okay, make that hot and humid) Florida, I've had many occasions to be grateful for the state's wonderful breezes. Sometimes gusty and sometimes gentle, sometimes crisp and sometimes warm, they always bring respite and the possibility of change. One of the wonderful aspects of Florida's breezes is that we don't have to work to enjoy them. No matter how distracted or harried we feel, we can always enjoy their coolness on our cheek or their promise of change.

In that same way, what I call "faith breezes" are small reminders of God that caress our souls and remind us that He is always near. No matter how small and delicate or big and gusty, a "faith breeze" connects us to all the great forces shaping life on Earth.

Faith breezes give us a glimpse of the awe-inspiring power of God. These reminders of glory stroke, and stoke, our faith. A memory of a coconut-head pirate from a childhood citrus stand... the bleak eyes of a parent slipping away into Alzheimer's disease....a grandchild's hilarious and surprisingly profound remark....a Biblical passage that strikes right to the heart of a struggle: all come at the exact right moment to remind us of God's presence...and all can be experienced and enjoyed in even our busiest moments. These moments of spiritual awareness are grounded with words from Scripture and passages from the writings of theologians, poets and authors.

Just as the breeze moves everything from the highest clouds to the lowest grains of sand, God's power breathes in all of the generations of human life. The brief pieces in Faith Breezes cover relationships that range from the bond with our elders to our connections with "grandbabies." Our primary relationship, that with God, runs through the book.

Throughout Faith Breezes, reflections on God, family and personal growth are woven together with passages of Scripture and brief vignettes from my own life. In sharing my own experiences, I speak as an "Everywoman" rather than an authority or expert. It is my hope that my times of struggle and moments of laughter will inspire you to celebrate the richness of your own life and the many ways God is present within it.

Thank you for being part of my journey, and for welcoming me into your own.

Sue Kennedy Holbrook
Vero Beach, Florida
March 2015

ABOUT THE BOOK

As women of faith, we sometimes take on too much. Our lives can easily become endless "to do" lists: each task important and worthwhile, but all of them together a constant struggle. I did not want to write a book that would give you more work. Like the breeze after which it is named, I wanted the book to feel like a series of small moments of refreshment...moments in which you can enjoy God's grace and stillness without effort, exertion or expectations.

With that in mind, I structured the book as a series of individual essays that can be approached in a variety of ways. You can read them in order or jump to a title that catches your interest. You can read them together or one piece at a time. You know what pace and sequence fit your situation, your needs, your longings and your life.

At the end of each essay, I have offered a reflection question and a lined journal page. Using these is entirely optional. See these reflection sections only as a gentle invitation to pause an extra moment in stillness if and when the spirit moves you. Here again, the best approach is simply that which suits your soul.

Except where otherwise noted, excerpts from Scripture are taken from the New International Version (NIV).

Spring

A GROUP OF GREATS

Listen to me, you who pursue righteousness and who seek the Lord:
look to the rock from which you were cut
and to the quarry from which you were hewn...
—Isaiah 51:1

FLORIDA'S CITRUS SEASON RUNS COUNTER TO THE GROWING cycle we expect from most other places and crops. Fall is usually thought of as a season of growth shutting down and dying off, but it's when the first oranges and grapefruit are coming out of the groves. By the time spring rolls around and the first growth is appearing elsewhere, the fruit packers are beginning to close down.

So yesterday, I slipped the lid off my last box of grapefruit for the season. Beautifully packed, it was a credit to anyone earning a living by putting fresh fruit into a carton—something I know from experience isn't as easy as it sounds.

Ah, I thought, *they're Flames.* Once you've seen the bright red pigment spotting the skin of the Red Flame, you'll never forget it.

Even better than the beautiful presentation is the smell. To me, the fragrance of grapefruit, just days away from being picked from the trees, is one of the cleanest, most appealing smells in the world.

Of course, I *would* love it. My entire life has been lived in and around the groves and packing houses where citrus is harvested and processed. As an adult, I spent a lot of years creating radio commercials and mail order catalogs, selling the fruits of my family's labors. But my work in citrus began long before that. This time of year, when those fragrances once again fill the air around me, I'm taken back to those early days. The sights, the smells, the tastes of grapefruit bring to mind the group of people who raised me.

Daddy and Mama were the nucleus of the group, but close around them were Uncle Tom—my father's older brother—and his wife, my Aunt Clyde. Not only did they live right across the street from each other, they all worked together in the family citrus business.

It was primarily a gift fruit business, with the grapefruit from our own groves at the core of its sales. We shipped gift packages of oranges and grapefruit all over the country. Our roadside shop—quaintly dubbed the "fruit stand," though it was actually a building—grew to be one of our city's most well-known and respected landmarks.

The most intense time of year was the first three weeks of December. It seemed to me as a child that everybody in the country wanted a basket of fruit delivered to somebody up North. Once the fruit was in them, we made the baskets festive for the holidays with red and green cellophane "grass" and fresh kumquats, their glossy green leaves still attached. The youngest worker—that was often me—was pressed into service throwing grass and kumquats in the top of the boxes and baskets that had

been packed by Aunt Clyde. When you're part of a family business, you learn never to say "I'm bored." Any time my mother
heard that, she said firmly "Come here." And your little self was
delegated a job without delay.

At 60-something, I can no longer sort out who in that group
of four had the most influence on me. They were all my authority
figures, and my brother Ken's as well. If one of the four adults
told us to do something, we did it. If they said stop it, we quit.
If they said "You're acting ugly," we straightened up. Or, at least,
we tried. My ideas about right and wrong, good and bad, decency,
fairness—my basic sense of how to treat people—were formed
by my group. In the words of that wise verse from Isaiah, they
were the rock from which I was hewn, and the world of Florida
citrus was the quarry from which I was cut.

One of the most important lessons I learned was that if you
want something bad enough, you keep working steadily toward
it. When it was the busy season—when the tourists were in town
in the winter months, *everybody* worked. Taking off for anything
short of being hospitalized was just not done. As Mama would
remind us every chance she got, "We've got to get it while it's
here!"

But what I hold most dear is the memory of the conversation
and fellowship that was such a constant in those working days.
We talked of things we wanted to do, places we wanted to go,
interesting things we wanted to see. We made plans to go shopping when time allowed. We dreamed of summer vacation trips
to far-off places we had only read about. A lot of what we wished
for eventually came to pass, but it didn't really matter—it was the
camaraderie that counted.

"How good and pleasant it is when brothers live together in

unity!" reads Psalm 133:1. That family business worked because of the unity of purpose of its core team. It wasn't the things they said but what they did that showed me their respect for each other and their commitment to honoring what God had given them. Our lives were shaped by their common mission just as surely as by Nature's growing and harvesting seasons—the rhythms of life set by God's creation.

Basking in the aura of that box of Red Flame grapefruit, I am back there in the fruit stand once again. The machinery is roaring as the fruit runs through it, Daddy is meticulously placing fruit in a mesh bag, Aunt Clyde is packing fruit into cartons, and Mama is arranging chocolate alligators on a table out front. Uncle Tom is coming in the back door with the crew, bringing in a fresh load of golden grapefruit.

If you'll allow me what sounds like a mixed metaphor, family strength, unity and citrus were the quarry and rock that formed me…and I thank God for all of them.

Feel the Breeze

What is the rock from which you were hewn and the quarry from which you were cut? What things remind you of the strengths these origins gave you?

MY CALLING

To serve the present age, my calling to fulfill...
O may it all my powers engage to do my Master's will.
—Charles Wesley, *A Charge to Keep I Have*

MY HIGH SCHOOL FRIENDS AND I MET RECENTLY AT A RESORT in the Georgia mountains. We had not been together in at least forty years. We hugged the years away amid the exclamations of "You look great! It's so good to see you!" We babbled over our buffet lunches like we had just talked last week.

As we shared what life has us doing now, I wondered how they would react to one of my pieces of news. Kids, grandkids, career achievements, travel: most of us have them. But spiritual experiences—how will people who knew you "back then" react when you share those?

Rather cautiously, I spoke about being called to preach. (Yeah, that's kind of a biggie.)

Kathy said thoughtfully, "Yes, that doesn't surprise me."

Well, it sure surprised *me*.

It was the spring of 2005. I settled into my seat in the choir loft and glanced casually at the church bulletin as I waited for the service to begin. The announcement that drew my attention said there would be a Basic Lay Speaker course taught at our church in just a few weeks. Anyone wishing to become a speaker could sign up in the church office.

I should explain right here that in the Methodist Church, trained lay people are often used to fill the pulpit in the pastor's absence and to speak in other capacities when called upon. For us, proclaiming Christ to the people is not the bailiwick of the ordained pastorate alone.

As I read that notice, there was a near-physical nudge from an unknown hand. I'd never experienced anything like that feeling before. At the same time, I heard a whisper in my innermost being: "This is for you. You need to do this."

Simultaneously, I stomped on my spiritual brakes. No way, no how! I was too busy. I was too old. I had plenty of projects and plenty of responsibilities. I didn't have the gifts or capacities or spiritual purity or depth of education needed.

I folded the bulletin and joined the Gathering Music, determined to forget the notice entirely.

But over the next three weeks, the inner battle continued. The notice kept appearing. I kept saying the same thing: *No, no, NO.* I thought at first that it was a battle between me and me. But then I realized that it was actually a battle between *God* and me.

Finally, I spoke to the pastor about it. Surely he would help me put my soul to rest with some really good and valid reasons not to take the course. He didn't. "I think you should do it," he calmly said. And walked away like it was simple and that was the end of it.

I prayed about it, I began to talk to Ed about it. I stewed on it. No matter what I said or thought or prayed, it wouldn't turn me loose. Finally, in desperation, I pointed my finger in God's direction. Of course, that could be any direction, since He's everywhere.

It was almost comic. I wagged my finger around authoritatively and explained my stipulations. "Okay, God...here's the deal. I will take the course, but ONLY so I can speak to women's groups. Do you hear that, God? Only for women. Never, NEVER in that pulpit in that sanctuary." God must have been rolling all over heaven laughing.

I took the course.

The first four times I spoke (even after ten years, I still have a hard time calling it preaching) were in that pulpit in that sanctuary. If I learned anything from this whole journey, it's this: don't give God an ultimatum, and don't tell Him what you won't do. It just amuses Him.

When I finally took the course, I was forced to face the fact that yes, there is a calling on my life, and yes, it is a serious one. It put my feet on a path I never dreamed I would travel.

In the end, it's simple. I can do nothing less than my best to fulfill the task laid out for me by the One who created me. God has given me the desire of my heart.

I now have the opportunity to share his messages with the women who come to the ladies' devotional lunch at my church. It is the highlight of my week. One of the ladies shared with me how difficult it would be for her to know she had to come up with a new message every week. Though I have the occasional dry spell, usually I can't wait to see what God is going to tell us next. I would run over hurdles to get there.

On occasion, I do get the call to fill the pulpit on Sunday. Being able to share God's word there is an honor I can't even describe.

The one who was most taken aback by this turn of events was Ed. He's been on this ride with me since day one. He never expected to be listening to me preach a sermon in church on Sunday in his twilight years. Neither did my brother. And neither did I.

Yet Kathy, who knew me mostly in my careless youth, *wasn't* surprised. It's good to know that one of the most surprising turns my life has taken seems logical to someone other than God!

Feel the Breeze

How does God call you to witness and share the Word in your own unique way? Are there changes you can make to better respond to his calling?

CAMEL. GOAT. WHATEVER.

This day is sacred to our Lord…
the joy of the Lord is your strength.
—Nehemiah 8:10

MY GRANDSON NATHANIEL'S FAVORITE WORD IS CURRENTLY AWESOME! I write it in all caps, with an exclamation point, because that's the way he says it: with so much enthusiasm you can't help but be excited along with him.

At this writing he's almost five and just the funniest kid. Each of the other three "grands" have their own personalities; every one is special and adorable in his/her own way. But then there's Nathaniel. So exuberant, such a lively little soul. You never have a clue what's coming out of his mouth next.

We recently visited the Knoxville Zoo together. It features a camel ride for young visitors. While cousins Andrew and Jack weren't interested—this was their own territory and they had ridden the beast before—Nathaniel and his sister, Charlotte, were more than up for the journey.

The camel caretakers hoisted them into the seats on the top of the hump and led them slowly around the ring. The children smiled all the way. I fulfilled a grandmother's role and snapped pictures to record the unusual scene.

At the end of the ride, the men picked the kids up again and set them on the platform.

Nathaniel came barreling down the ramp. At the top of his lungs he yelled, "That was AWESOME! I never rode a goat before!"

A laugh rippled through the crowd. As the oft-used expression has it, they were definitely laughing with him, not at him. His joy was infectious.

Goat. Camel. Whatever. He might not have known his animals, but Nathaniel knew the truth. Accuracy about the species didn't matter to him.

For him, it was only the delight that counted.

As adults, it's surprisingly easy to talk ourselves out of joy. *Sure, the sunset is beautiful—but it's going to rain tomorrow. Of course the car is running great—but but it's not the latest model. The kids love this zoo—but there's a better one across the state.*

We often get so analytical about the details that we miss the joy they're supposed to be giving us.

Accuracy, realism, awareness, knowledge, the distinction between one thing and another: they're all important. But sometimes we need to set all of them aside and simply enjoy the animal we're riding on, no matter what its name may be.

"You still haven't ridden a goat, Nathaniel. That was a camel," we tried to explain, but he was too busy. He shrugged his shoulders as he put his lanky body in gear, heading off to find the next adventure of discovery. "Otters, Mimi?" he asked me. "What's an otter?"

Well, let's just go find out. Another discovery, another joy in this great world God created.

Feel the Breeze

What joys and delights offer themselves to you today? What caveats and conditions could you set aside to revel in them more fully?

A DIRECT MESSAGE

*On one occasion, while he was eating with them, he gave them this
command: "Do not leave Jerusalem, but wait for the gift my Father
promised, which you have heard me speak about."*
—Acts 1:4

ANSWERS TO PRAYERS ARE SOMETIMES VERY DIRECT AND UN-
expected. And brief, and to the point. Like this morning.

Our family has been praying fervently about a certain situation
for some months. It seems like God has forgotten us.

Again this morning, as I picked up my Bible and started my
day, my spirit was in that pleading mode. "God, you know what
is needed. Please bring relief soon!"

I opened my Bible to the first chapter of Acts. And right there
it was, in verse 4.

But wait. That's what it said. *But wait.* Jesus was telling the
disciples that the Holy Spirit—the gift God had promised them—
would become apparent in a few days.

The two words jumped out at me this morning because some-
time ago, years ago, I had underlined just those two words.

But wait.

I don't know why. Did God know I would need that message
at some future time?

I'm learning not to over-think these little gifts of encouragement.

I didn't need to understand.

I just needed to obey.

It was right there on the page.

And so I will…just wait.

Feel the Breeze

What are you waiting for today? How can you support yourself—through prayer, readings of Scripture, the comfort of friends—as you wait?

_____

_____

_____

_____

_____

_____

_____

_____

_____

A WOMAN NAMED CLYDE

And who knoweth whether thou art come to the Kingdom
for such a time as this?
—Esther 4:14 KJV

STEPPING THROUGH THE GATE, I MADE MY WAY AROUND THE pool, through the sliding door and into the family room. As usual, she was sitting in the big recliner, her permanent spot when she was not in bed. Her legs were propped up and she waved the TV remote in her hand. She was glad to see me, just as I was glad to see her.

I can't begin to fathom what my life would have been like without my Aunt Clyde. That's right...a woman named Clyde. It's a funny name for a funny woman, and she appreciated the joke.

Having someone close to me who represented fun and laughter made all the difference in my life when I was young. Not that my parents were totally dour. They wanted fun and they did laugh, but it didn't come readily to them. Our family needed somebody to lead us to lightheartedness and joy.

And that somebody came to us when Daddy's brother, Uncle Tom, married Clyde. Tom and Clyde never had children, but they had a passel of nieces and nephews who loved being in their presence and in their home. How fully they allowed us—indeed, welcomed us—to pass in and out of their home (just across the street from our own) amazes me to this day. It was rare that we were sent home or that a door was locked, which gives you an idea of their love and patience.

Traveling with them, too, was a treat not to be missed. Clyde's motto, quoted often in this book: "Everything's an adventure!"

Clyde was the antithesis of my mother. Mom was intense, strong willed, and always working. She had little time or attention for things like books, movies, sports and TV shows. Clyde , on the other hand, let herself enjoy such frivolities. She worked as hard as anyone when she worked—but when she was finished, she was ready to have fun.

Even better, she shared that fun with us. I'll never forget when Tom and Clyde got a TV. It was the early 1950s, so our neighborhood still had very few sets. With Clyde, I reveled in the exciting world of *The Honeymooners, Topper,* and *I've Got a Secret.* Those hours were filled with laughter, camaraderie, and relaxation. There was no judgment and no pressure to do anything but sit and enjoy.

I've reveled in Clyde's sense of adventure as an adult. But I think it was in childhood that I needed it the most. Being so "in the moment" themselves, kids crave the presence of people like Clyde and the sense of wonder and magic those folks bring with them.

At the visit I described at the opening of this piece, Clyde was 91, a widow, and housebound, helped by 'round the clock aides. But before a badly broken ankle that refused to heal kept her at home, she saw most of the major sights of the world.

It was because of Clyde that I saw Rome, experiencing the

glories of St. Peter's and the Sistine Chapel. And it's probably because of her that I can enjoy more mundane pleasures, too—a good book or a deliciously bad television show—and sit still long enough to feel the glory of God's creation.

Since I first wrote this piece, Clyde has passed on. But she lives on in my memory and, I hope, my spirit.

Thanks, Clyde. I know in my heart you came for such a time as this.

Feel the Breeze

Whether it is a spouse, a relative, a friend, even an animal companion, who adds zest to your life, helps you savor the many delights of God's world?

SALTY SERVICE

Jesus said, "You are the salt of the earth."
—Matthew 5:13

If Christ lives in us, controlling our personalities,
we will leave glorious marks on the lives we touch.
Not because of our character but because of His.
—Eugenia Price

SALT. IT'S SO FAMILIAR WE RARELY THINK ABOUT IT.

White table salt used to be the only kind you could find. Now popular salts come from all around the world and are as varied as the world's peoples: Hawaiian Black Lava and Red Alaea Sea Salt, Himalayan Pink Mountain Salt, light grey Celtic Sea Salt, darker grey Spanish Sea Salt and white Dead Sea Salt. Different natural salts have different mineral profiles depending on their source, giving each one a unique flavor and color.

Saltiness is one of the basic taste sensations, one of the oldest of food seasonings, and the best known of food preservatives. Down through time, salt has been a trading commodity or currency, a healing balm and a cleansing agent. Salt was held in such high esteem by the ancient Hebrews that they had a Covenant of Salt with God. Salt was sprinkled on their offerings to show

23

their trust in God…a fitting use of an essential element of life on this earth.

Metaphorically, we are salt in the Kingdom of God: our service is essential to sustaining, preserving, and growing the kingdom. But just what do we mean by acts of "salty service"? It can be anything that uses your life to make the world a better place and shares the love that Jesus lived out before us. Jesus said we are all salt, no matter what our colors or nationalities or other differences. So our ways of doing "salty service" can be different too.

Holding out our hand to share the love of Christ to someone who needs it…teaching His Word to those who have never heard… writing a poem of praise or singing a song of thanks to the Creator: your service will be unique to you.

Salty service means flavoring the world around you with your love and good works.

It's what you do that only you can do, in Jesus's name.

Feel the Breeze

Like salt, service to God comes in many varieties. What is the "flavor" of your own personal kind of salty service?

ONE GREAT TRIP

Perfect love sometimes does not come until the first grandchild.
—Welsh proverb

THE BOX OF OLD PAPERS WAS YIELDING NOTHING OF INTEREST. Most of what I had seen was now in the garbage bag at my feet. I almost dropped the strip of heavy paper into the trash before I realized it looked official. When I looked more closely, I realized that it was a train ticket dated March 30, 1944, from Vero Beach, Florida, to Big Spring, Texas.

It might not mean much to someone else. But I understand how much it signifies.

It was my grandmother's passage for a three day train ride taken to welcome me—her first grandchild—into the world. Though I've lived virtually all my life in Florida, I was actually born in Texas. She traveled all that distance to be there at my birth, going all by herself and at a cost of $66—not a small sum in those days.

My maternal grandmother, known to us kids as Mema Jessie, lived to the ripe old age of 90. By today's standards, her world was small and restricted. She rarely left Vero Beach. When she did, it was for short day trips—at most, the occasional journey to

26

visit family in Georgia. The only thing that ever moved her to venture farther from home than that was my birth. The train, which ran right outside her door, took her all the way to the west side of Texas to a town called Big Spring. She talked about it for the rest of her life—it was clearly a highlight for her. She never once flew on an airplane, but I apparently gave her one heck of a train trip!

Vero Beach, Florida, and Big Spring, Texas, are light years apart in character. Vero Beach has palm trees and oak trees. Big Spring has mesquite bushes and tumbleweeds. The climate, the accents, the lifestyles are completely different. I can't begin to fathom the culture shock my grandmother experienced when she stepped off that train.

It was World War II that necessitated the trip to Texas. Wartime had displaced the whole world; soldiers and their wives were living in whatever quarters they could find. By the time I was about to make my appearance, my parents' home was a converted tourist court called Camp Dixie. In the fashion of the day, a tourist court was a group of small cottages that was the forerunner of the post-war motel. Mama often described their move to Camp Dixie as stepping up to a mansion. Before Camp Dixie, my parents had lived in one room, rented from a kindly family who allowed Mama to use their kitchen from time to time. She was grateful for their many favors to a homesick young couple—but even though it was one big room with a hot plate for a kitchen, just having their own space was next to heaven.

I was late in coming. (Perhaps that set the tone for my lifelong time challenges.) Mema Jessie spent about six weeks in Big Spring due to my tardy arrival. She didn't like being so far away from her beloved Charlie, but she would have put up with anything to help her young daughter to settle in with her new baby.

I've often wondered what in the world she did in the ten days or so that Mama was in the hospital. Daddy worked long hours at the Army base. The only available transportation was the city bus line which scared her to death. It didn't matter that there was no car. Mema Jessie had never learned to drive, so she couldn't have used it anyway. I guess she busied herself doing whatever baby preparations still needed to be made, along with the normal chores of keeping house.

Mema loved to tell me about the day she got up the nerve to ride the bus to town by herself. She used the trip to buy some lace for the trim of a dress she was making for me, the new arrival. Wouldn't you know, a dust storm blew up out of nowhere as she stood on the corner waiting for the bus. The bag with the precious lace was blown from her hand, never to be seen again.

That trip to Texas was just the beginning of Mema Jessie's reign as a grandmother. She created a warm and welcoming home where all of her grandchildren were cherished. Because my parents soon moved back to Vero Beach and she lived such a long life, not only my brother and I and our three cousins but also our children got to bask in her special attention.

More than any other of my forebears, Jessie was to her family the embodiment of unconditional love. She loved us with good cooking—her cathead biscuits were legendary—and she loved us with her open arms. Her door was open any hour of the day or night. She never traveled so far alone again, but I have no doubt that she would have if she was needed.

When it comes to grandmothering, Mema Jessie had a long run. And it all started with a train trip to Big Spring, Texas.

Feel the Breeze

How do the stories of your arrival remind you of your family's love, faith and strength?

_____

_____

_____

_____

_____

_____

_____

_____

_____

ON FAITH AND FRIENDSHIP

When your devotion draws you
down a difficult way,
may you know
the friendship of Christ
who goes with you.
—Jan Richardson, *In the Sanctuary of Women*

FRIENDS FOR MORE THAN FORTY YEARS, JUDY AND I ARE A great lesson that friends don't have to be cut off the same pattern. Their personalities can be as opposite as daylight and dark, and their likes and dislikes can be just as different.

I really noticed this recently when we had lunch at the Cheesecake Factory. Our entrees were done. Now we sat with our coffee. Judy pored over the cheesecake menu. I didn't know what she would select, but I knew her choice would be the opposite of mine. She wanted hers with all the gunk and goo, flavor and spice they could put in it—the goopier the better. I didn't need a menu. I just wanted cheesecake. No pumpkin added, not even a drop of chocolate sauce or strawberries. Simple and plain. Just...cheesecake.

We're the same way with coffee. Hers has to be sweetened

and creamed. Mine has to be black. Don't mess up my coffee. Or my tea.

As you can tell, she likes life dressed up, blinged and bangled to the max. I'll take it plain and simple, please.

Our differences aren't just trivial things. A few years back, our friendship was shaken. Critical changes occurred in the life of our church, and each of us—with our families—were led in different directions as we sought a new church home. It wouldn't have been so painful if we'd always attended different churches. It was the sudden dividing of our paths that felt painful and scary.

We wondered if we could bridge this gap. Those around us weren't optimistic. But though the road was bumpy at times, our respect for our friendship and our common love for the Lord and for his work—wherever that might take us—proved equal to the challenge.

In fact, that time of difference has led both of us to areas of growth we never saw coming. Even our occasionally fiery theological discussions have taught us valuable lessons. Sometimes we must simply agree to disagree. We've learned to accept that, though perhaps we might not have managed it so well when we first met as young women. Maturity has its advantages.

Seeing things of the Lord differently is not new and certainly not unique to Judy and me. When Paul wrote his letter to the church at Philippi, he called out two women who were obviously going at it in the name of Jesus. "I plead with Euodia and I plead with Syntyche to agree with each other in the Lord," he said. And in Philippians 4:2-3, he asks the others in the church to "help these women who have contended at my side in the cause of the gospel..."

Contend in the cause of the gospel. I like that phrase. Sometimes Judy and I do just that. Sometimes it's difficult to find a place of agreement. But we both know the friendship of Christ—both with each other and with Him. For the sake of the gospel, we keep our focus on the One who is the common denominator for everything we do. As Paul said in his letter to the Colossians: "He is before all things, and in him all things hold together."

All things hold together. Even two Christian women who don't agree on cheesecake, but love each other as sisters in the Lord.

What's important is not our differences. It's this: we both know that in the gospel kingdom, we each have a place, and we matter.

Our friend, Jesus, assures us that we do.

Feel the Breeze

Where do you have differences—about faith, or anything else—with your own friends? How does He help you find resolution?

_____

_____

_____

_____

_____

_____

_____

_____

_____

_____

GRANDMOTHER'S FAITH

I am reminded of your sincere faith, a faith that lived first in your
grandmother Lois and your mother Eunice and now, I am sure,
lives in you. For this reason I remind you to rekindle the gift of God
that is within you through the laying on of my hands; for God did not
give us a spirit of cowardice, but rather a spirit of power and of love
and of self-discipline.
—2 Timothy 1:5-7 MSG

I LOOKED ACROSS THE TABLE AT MY FIRSTBORN GRANDCHILD.
Andrew is tall and slender, with brown hair and blue eyes. A good
looking young man, if Mimi does say so herself. The shadow
across his upper lip and the hoarse, deep tones coming when he
speaks tell me he's not a little boy anymore. In fact, as I write
this, he will be 16 in just a few weeks.

I want him to grow up—you always want them to grow up—
but grandmothers don't always deal with these things very well.

When our lunch was delivered, Andrew's father suggested he
say grace for us. We all bowed and waited patiently. Andrew's
voice is soft and his speech rapid, so we had to listen carefully as
he prayed. He had a lot to say to God even if those around the
table couldn't make out every word. But I know that prayer went
straight from his lips to God's ears because Andrew is an intense

straight-shooter. He has Asperger's syndrome, which creates challenges. We've all had to learn how to deal with those and to give him the space he needs to be able to function. But we've also learned from him.

I don't remember exactly what Andrew prayed that day, but I know he prayed for all of us in clear terms. He has a gift of God that is within him. I recall several years ago being very concerned about him. I prayed fervently for God to help Andrew find his way through the maze of nagging issues that constantly beset him. That's one time in my life that my answer from God was immediate and almost audible.

I've got him. He's mine. Trust me.

And so I stand on this Scripture that we don't have a spirit of fear. It's very clear that he has given Andrew a spirit of power and love. And he's learning self-discipline.

Hopefully, so are we.

Feel the Breeze

What Scriptures do you keep stored in your memory to help dispel your fears? When has God spoken directly to your heart in times of challenge?

OLD AGE, GRAY HAIRS & BEARING FRUIT

So even to old age and gray hairs, O God, do not forsake me,
until I proclaim your might to another generation,
your power to all those to come.
—Psalm 71:18

I AM NOW MUCH MORE SENIOR THAN I EVER THOUGHT ABOUT being. I have attended my 50-year high school reunion. Only old people do that.

Today my husband and I are eating dinner in a local restaurant. It's only six o'clock or so, and apparently the young, hip crowd—if there is such a thing in our Florida town—doesn't appear this early. All around us sit folks with gray hair, or glasses, or both. The only young faces in the place are the servers and the occasional grandchild.

"I see these people and they look so old," my husband, Ed, said to me. "And then I realize they look just like me."

I think that Ed looks wonderful for his age. But then, I'm partial. And there's no doubt that however young we may or may not look, we're right there in the same age range as all of the other seniors sitting around us.

When you live, like we do, in Florida, you get plenty of occasions like this, when you can muse on the word "senior." Having pondered the aging process—and it's not an elective, it's a required subject when you're as old as I am—I have decided that for me at least, being senior doesn't mean the game is over, or even in the fourth quarter, the bottom of the ninth, or the last lap.

Instead, I find it's a time that's as full of urgent questions as young people are full of boundless energy.

What have you done in your life? What experiences have you gathered up? What have you learned that you need to share with those around you…your family, your friends, your church? What do you still need to learn? Do you think God means for you or me or anybody else to just quit?

Some of my inspiration for this comes from Psalm 92:

The righteous will flourish like a palm tree,
they will grow like a cedar of Lebanon;
planted in the house of the Lord,
they will flourish in the courts of our God.
They will still bear fruit in old age,
they will stay fresh and green,
proclaiming, "The Lord is upright;
he is my Rock, and there is no wickedness in him."

If we plant ourselves in God's word and in his house, we will continue to grow. What's more, we will bear fruit in our old age—stay fresh and green! We might not look like a glossy young sprout, but we can continue to share Jesus with those around us in some form or fashion.

In the material world, this is the stage of life when we're all "used to be's." We all used to be something. Faster, healthier, prettier. I used to have hips that didn't hurt, feet that walked

better, a face that wasn't so wrinkled, hair that wasn't...oops...
don't go there!

But in God's eyes, of course, things are different. Whatever
I used to be, I am—we are—still important in God's kingdom
today. And I still have work that He expects me to do. I am here
to affirm: the Lord is upright. He is my rock.

In the words of another majestic psalm, I intend to proclaim
His might to another generation.

But that's for tomorrow. Tonight I'm just going to sit here
with my gracefully aging husband and let some energetic young-
sters deliver our dessert.

Feel the Breeze

Whether you're about my age or in some entirely different stage of life, how are you serving and gaining strength from God as you grow older?

THE "W" WORD

Do all the good you can, by all the means you can, in all the ways you can, in all the places you can, at all the times you can, to all the people you can, as long as ever you can.

—John Wesley

THE FOUNDER OF THE METHODIST CHURCH, JOHN WESLEY, had no thought of founding a new denomination of Christianity. He just wanted to see the Church of England become more spirit-filled—more responsive to the needs of the people of his time. The Church wasn't interested in his approach.

So Wesley took his message of salvation and hope to the streets and the fields of England. When there was no one else to preach to the people, he called on whoever was grounded in the faith to carry the word...including women.

In a period when women were mostly seen as extensions of the men to whom they were attached, his decision was highly controversial. His willingness to let women preachers help carry the message was denounced far and wide by his time's religious leaders. Among other things, they felt that descendents of Eve weren't pure enough to spread the word.

Wesley persisted in the face of opposition. Many came to know Christ in a personal way because some woman from the local congregation stood under a tree in the middle of a field and shared salvation with them.

I have been encouraged and uplifted by the stories I've read about these women from the 1700s, a time when women had little power and less voice.

My favorite anecdote from the time is this. A woman wrote Mr. Wesley asking him to reassure her that it was acceptable for her to preach. His response to her was simple. "Sister, do all the good you can."

That simple sentence is the crux of the calling for me and, I suspect, for all those who are believers who carry the message of Christ. For me, for you, wherever we speak it. In our homes, in our workplace, during our leisure, as we serve in our churches. Whatever our calling in life may be.

And whatever our gender may be, too.

My life as a lay preacher has been shaped by those two "w" words: Wesley, and woman. And by Wesley's conviction that women are God's children—and messengers—right along with men.

But whether or not you are called to preach, I echo Wesley's beautiful words.

Sister, do all the good you can.

Feel the Breeze

How could you release society's expectations of how we should behave as women to more fully follow your inner calling or God's vision for you?

SNOWED IN...IN ALABAMA

The prudent see danger and take refuge,
but the simple keep going and suffer for it.
—Proverbs 27:12

Whoever is wise, let him heed these things
and consider the great love of the Lord.
—Psalm 107:43

IT WAS A TIME WHEN WE SHOULD HAVE HEEDED ALL THE WARN-ings of danger. But we didn't.

It was the middle of March, 1993. A snowstorm was the last thing Ed and I expected to experience. Our younger daughter, Becky—then a student at Samford University in Birmingham, Alabama—was scheduled to present her junior voice recital on Monday evening. As any parent of a musician knows, this is a big deal.

On Thursday afternoon, Ed and I were working as hard as we could to get on the road for Birmingham. March is the middle of "the Season" in Vero Beach and the drugstore we owned at the time was a madhouse. Our bags were packed and waiting at home. Our plan was to be on the road by late afternoon. We would spend the night somewhere in Georgia, arriving at Becky's dorm by early afternoon Friday. Plenty of time to help with her recital gown and accessories and wrap up the catering details for the reception.

In the midst of the chaos at the pharmacy, my mother called.

"Have you all looked at the weather?" she asked, her voice tight with nerves.

It was a sunny 80 degrees outside. No. I had not seen the national weather.

"Well, you better look," she warned. "There's a bad storm coming across the South. It's going to be really bad by morning."

Mama had a history of exaggerating weather details. So I simply thanked her and assured her we would be gone soon.

I recalled that conversation many times over the next 48 hours. She had not exaggerated. Blustery wind gave way to misting rain that turned into sleet and finally blowing snow. We left our warm safe motel room in Albany, Georgia, during the misting rain phase, still not realizing how dire the weather forecast was. I should add that Ed and I are both natives of the deep South. We had no experience of snow, and those who don't know snow are not prudent in the face of it.

There was no way to turn back. We pressed on through hours and hours of scary, heart-pounding, snow-blinded travel over a desolate road. Any moment could have turned disastrous, even life-threatening, in the blink of an eye. We learned later that shortly after we turned onto this particular stretch of highway, the Alabama Highway Patrol closed the road. We were out there all alone.

Well—not quite all alone. As Psalm 107:26-28 describes, "In their peril, their courage melted away. They reeled and staggered like drunken men; they were at their wit's end. Then they cried out to the Lord in their trouble, and he brought them out of their distress."

We prayed to Him. And he did bring us out of our distress. We crept along in the snow until we finally reached Sylacauga, which had an exit road we were able to maneuver. All motel rooms there were full. Then we encountered a sweet young couple who saved us with their generosity. Their offer to share their room that had two beds was gratefully accepted. We hated to inconvenience them, but we were out of options.

That small motel room became our world for the next 24 hours. The restaurant was closed and the vending machines were running low. However, our friends had a loaf of bread, a dozen eggs and a quart jar of homemade vegetable beef soup. We had a bag of oranges and grapefruit, instant coffee and tea bags, and a small travel pot for heating water.

Even though power was out at the buildings all around us, our room never lost it. We always had hot water. We always had heat. We always had some sort of TV reception. We boiled eggs, heated soup and made coffee in the travel pot. We talked. TV kept us updated on conditions across the state. As we learned the details of other people stranded by the storm—with medical emergencies and homes with inside temps in the 20s—we knew we were in great shape.

When the road finally cleared, we went on to Birmingham to check on Becky. She was fine but campus was shut down. We turned our faces south and went home, all the way marveling that we had been snowed in...in Sylacauga, Alabama of all places!

We had barely cleared the door when Becky called us.

"They've rescheduled my recital for Monday," she exclaimed. "You've got to come back!"

I can only ruefully echo the verse of Scripture quoted at the start of this essay: *Whoever is wise, let him heed these things and consider the great love of the Lord.*

Feel the Breeze

How has the Lord brought you out of distress or even danger?

_____

_____

_____

_____

_____

_____

_____

_____

_____

A SHINING LIGHT

You are the light of the world…let your light shine before men, that
they may see your good deeds and praise your Father in heaven.
—Matthew 5:16

THE GREY-HAIRED LADY HOBBLED DOWN THE SIDEWALK, WAVING at us as she went. "Thanks for coming! See you later."

She had all the panache of someone climbing aboard a Harley as she got into the seat of her scooter. With another wave of her hand and a big smile on her face, she hit the gas and took off. The small American flag mounted on the back flapped in the breeze.

"My gosh!" Ed exclaimed. "I didn't know that thing would go that fast." The woman driving was his mother, Rachael. We had just finished lunch at the retirement center where she lives, about a mile from our house. It was a celebration lunch, held every month for those having birthdays. She was turning 91. And she is still the symbol of independence and determination in our family. She is truly a "doer."

Ed is her only child. Rachael has now outlived all of her siblings. The last one, her twin sister, passed in May. Since I've been in her family for the past 40-plus years, I've seen her have the ups and downs that life brings to all of us in one form or another.

She was widowed by the time she was 50. She cared for three of her sisters until, one by one, they passed away. How many twins do you know that live to be 90? She shared with me one day that this birthday would be hard because it was the first one in her life without Mary. I've seen her in sick times and healthy times, peaceful times and times of extreme stress. Through it all, I've known her to be a person of great faith and resilience.

After her husband died, Rachael lived alone in Naples, Florida, the other side of the state from us. This worked until health issues made us all begin to discuss the realities of her future in a town where she had no close family. Friends are great, and she has some good ones. But we're her caretakers and she needed to be near us. Like the independent person she is, Rachael herself made the decision to move to the retirement center near our home. She wanted to make the move on her own terms, not wait until we would have to do it for her.

It was following that move that we watched her sink into a dark time. Adjusting to a form of semi-communal living was tough, although there are many "positives." She has a lovely duplex apartment that overlooks a lake. The campus of the center is peaceful with oak trees dripping with moss. She can cook, or have her meals in the dining room. And there are people around to make friends with. The downside—the people are more mature and often a bit infirm and she was not accustomed to having the age issue right in her face daily.

It took her several months, but gradually the "doer" came out. Somewhere in the center of her being, Rachael stepped into the meaning of that old song: "This little light of mine, I'm gonna let it shine." As she acclimated to the new place and got to know her neighbors and the staff, she once again became the helper she has always been. Her only physical issue is those bad knees that keep her from walking around like she loves to do. Enter the scooter. It takes her every place she wants to go on the campus. She also has her car, but she only drives as far as WalMart.

The center offers a variety of activities for the residents and she has offered her help in many ways. In fact, two years ago, she was named Volunteer of the Year. She is one of those people for whom the term "faith warrior" was coined. Isn't it encouraging to see energetic women of faith still serving the Lord in their years of maturity? It lets all of us know that these things we call faith and hope are valid and truly hold us up in all seasons of our lives.

Feel the Breeze

"Faith warriors" are all around us, if we only look to see them. Who are the faith warriors that encourage your life?

_____

_____

_____

_____

_____

_____

_____

_____

_____

_____

UNDER HIS FEET

Upon that cross of Jesus
Mine eye at times can see
The very dying form of One
Who suffered there for me;
And from my stricken heart with tears
Two wonders I confess:
The wonders of redeeming love
And my unworthiness.
—Elizabeth C. Clephane

"LORD, TEACH US TO PRAY." THE DISCIPLES WERE SEEKING Jesus's wisdom when it comes to being in God's presence. And Jesus gave them that beautiful example prayer that we all repeat so often. That's a great beginning. But prayer is so much more.

Books on how to pray have been written by the millions. The thing is…we're all so different. And we communicate in so many different ways. God knows that. If we can talk to our best earthly friend, we can talk to God. Quite frankly, God knows that if I try to follow someone else's prayer formula, it just won't be *me*.

God is spirit and they that worship him must worship him in spirit and in truth. The truth of my spirit is that I very often just need to visualize things. Sometimes, I listen to the sound effects of waves washing on the shore. Jesus takes my hand and we walk and talk. Sometimes we sit by the shore in companionable silence.

Distress always sends me to the foot of the cross, under his feet. I can look up into his eyes as he was in such torment and know that he knows my pain, too.

Not long ago, I heard someone say something I've heard so many times in my life. "Leave your cares and concerns at the foot of the cross."

Right then, I was most distressed with someone in my life. I thought about that saying all day. That night when I closed my eyes to meditate and pray, I found myself wrapping that person up like a bundle. I could see myself carrying my bundle up a hill. When I got to the foot of the cross, I set it on the ground.

"There! It's Yours. I've done all I can!"

And I left it there. I know I may have to take it back there at some future time, but that's okay.

Since that first time, I've left a few other problems there at the foot of the cross. I've even thrown myself down right there a few times.

To me, this is the most intimate form of prayer: to practice being in the presence of God through the sacrifice of His son.

Come and join me—under his feet.

Feel the Breeze

Is there a care or burden you need to set at his feet today?

_____

_____

_____

_____

_____

_____

_____

_____

_____

_____

A MOMENT OF TOOTH

Humble yourselves, therefore, under God's mighty hand,
that he may lift you up in due time.
Cast all your anxiety on him because he cares for you.
—1 Peter 5:6-7

"CHARLOTTE'S COMING UP THE BACK STAIRS WITH BLOOD coming out of her mouth!"

The one shouting those words was grandson Jack. His cry set three women into "warp speed," headed for the kitchen door.

With all four of their children safely occupied, my daughters Lyn and Becky had been enjoying a rare moment of girl time with me. Of course, the phrases "young children" and "safely occupied" don't truly go together. What had we been thinking? While Andrew and Nathaniel were playing a game in the basement, Jack and Charlotte had gone out to jump on the trampoline. Now, Emergency was coming up the back steps.

Lyn opened the door. Jack wasn't kidding. The child had her hand over her mouth and the red stuff was dripping. She was huffing and puffing and wailing with every step.

No granny can bear for her babes to be sick or get hurt. I've rocked all of my four "grands" through some sicknesses, but I've missed most of the accidents. I wasn't there the day Andrew flipped off the couch and hit the coffee table and busted his head open. I wasn't there the day Jack slammed the door on his fingers at day care and had to have his hand sewn up. I wasn't there the day Andrew drove a little John Deere truck off the driveway ledge and Jack's chin took the brunt of the fall.

Today, I *was* there. And even worse than a rough-and-tumble boy, it was my little granddaughter that was hurting. It took everything I had not to throw up. Or at the very least sit down and have a heart attack.

And it got worse. Charlotte's front tooth was gone. Becky and Lyn raced out to find it.

I grabbed Charlotte and held her as tight as I could. She was shaking and hysterical. After a few minutes of pressing a paper towel onto the hole in her gum to stop the bleeding, I got brave and decided to see for myself if the whole thing was really gone. Oh, yeah. Wish I hadn't done that.

My looking made Charlotte want to see. I calmly talked her out of it. At one point, Lyn made the mistake of saying "Well, maybe it was a baby tooth."

"No it wasn't!" Charlotte wailed. I guess when it's part of your own body, distinctions like that don't mean much.

And then she cried some more.

Lyn was on the phone with the children's dentist. I had never met the man, but he was sent from God that day. I know it's his job to be calm in such a crisis, but he did that job to the max for us.

"How long do we have while you're still at the office?" Lyn asked.

"Until you get here."

"What if we don't find it?"

"Bring her here anyway. We're going to do something for this child tonight one way or the other."

By now Charlotte was wandering the yard aimlessly, crying and bewailing the loss of a part of herself. "It's gone. We'll never find it. It won't matter. It's out now, never coming back. Adios, tooth!"

We did find the tooth. It was sitting up on a tuft of grass, like a golf ball on a tee. As instructed, we placed it, root and all, in a small container of milk. Apparently the root cells needed for it to reattach would be washed away in water but are safe in milk. Ah, the things a grandmother learns.

We were further blessed that the dentist stayed open, the tooth was reattached, and it's still nice and white like it's supposed to be.

Being a woman of faith doesn't mean you don't get the shakes when a crisis hits. Especially when it hits your little ones. Fear and anxiety about the outcome are very real. We know down deep inside that what lies ahead could be—and often is—truly unpleasant, that it may test our faith far more than we want to be tested. As humans, we're scared...we're sad...we hurt. That's when we do our best to cast our anxieties on the One who has promised to help us bear them.

Teeth are not always found. Children are not always healed and healthy, at least not in this life. But whatever the outcome, God is there. "I will never leave you or forsake you," says Joshua 1:5. "Fear not, for I have redeemed you; I have called you by name; you are mine. When you pass through the waters, I will be with you," reads Isaiah 43:1-2.

His promises hold true. He is there. Even when you're shaking uncontrollably in a dentist's office, with a wailing child at your side and a tooth in your hand.

Feel the Breeze

When have you felt God's presence beside you in a crisis?

_____

_____

_____

_____

_____

_____

_____

_____

_____

Summer

ACCEPTING THE ADVENTURE

Then they said to him, "Please inquire of God to learn whether our journey will be successful." The priest answered them, "Go in peace. Your journey has the Lord's approval."
—Judges 18:5-6

Everything's an adventure.
—Clyde Kennedy

THE VERSES FROM JUDGES 18 QUOTED ABOVE TALK ABOUT getting the Lord's approval for our journeys.

I can't say for sure. But I suspect that many or most of our journeys have the Lord's approval when we make them with a willingness to accept what he, rather than a travel agent, has planned for us.

The Bible has numerous lessons about that kind of acceptance. My Aunt Clyde taught me something about it as well.

As I mentioned earlier, Clyde taught me how to travel. I mean that literally; some of my earliest travels were taken with my parents, my brother, Aunt Clyde and Uncle Tom. I got most of my sense of how to act on the road *and* most of my sense of the majesty of God's wide world at her side.

But those words are also true on a deeper level. Clyde

understood the nature of travel: the ups and downs, the disappointments and delights, the need for energy and adaptability and acceptance. Traveling with her, you couldn't help but grasp that no matter how wonderful a trip might be, it wouldn't reflect the glossy tourist brochures. She knew, and communicated through her every action, that perfection wasn't the point. As I've noted before, "Everything's an adventure" was Clyde's most-often-repeated mantra. She would laugh as she added, "It might be a good adventure, it might be a bad adventure. But it's an adventure." And whatever the flaws or even calamities of the last journey, she was always planning her next trip.

I've been beside Clyde in Rome and London and Las Vegas. But the picture of Clyde that will always remain in my head is of her seated comfortably in a leather lounge chair in front of huge picture windows watching our ship pass through the Panama Canal. She was elderly by then, and not very mobile at all. Ed and I were the ones to run all over the ship, catching the details of the locks and watching for the sights on the shore. We left the big comfy seats for those more infirm than we were, who needed them. Out of necessity, Clyde stayed put. But crossing the Panama Canal was one of the things on her bucket list; she was determined to do it, and we were privileged to share it with her.

She took in every detail of the crossing, which is a long one. We started through the canal shortly after 8 a.m. and sailed into the Pacific Ocean about 3 p.m. Along the way, Ed and I took her some lunch and held her seat so she could take a restroom break without losing her front-row seat.

To be there—to experience the place she had read about—that's what Clyde wanted. Even if she experienced it from a chair. It was an adventure, unforgettable *and* comfortable.

Rick Warren, pastor and author of *The Purpose Driven Life,* comments that he used to think life was a series of peaks and valleys, ups and downs. After living for quite a few years, he has realized that the good and bad of life run on parallel tracks. Every situation will have bits of each.

I think he's right. Certainly, the many travels I've been privileged to make—with and without Clyde—demonstrate the truth of the comment. Fulfilling the yearning I had always had to see Lake Maggiore (if you've seen the 1962 film *Rome Adventure,* starring Troy Donohue and Suzanne Pleshette, you may understand why)...only to have Ed twist his knee on a cobblestone street only a few days into the trip.

As we doggedly followed our itinerary, Ed's knee got steadily worse. Como, Milan, Venice...his pain increased with every step. He had to endure agony. I had to put on my "big girl panties," do some exploring by myself, and make new friends without my security-blanket and best friend Ed reassuringly at my side.

> Going to the Costa del Sol to play golf—only to discover that the airline had lost every bit of our luggage except Ed's golf bag. As we learned, you can't wear a five iron, and golf towels don't cover much.

> Enjoying Edinburgh—but missing the turkey and dressing we would normally have been eating on that particular Thursday in November.

> Walking towards Gaudi's masterpiece, the Familia Sagrada cathedral, in the soulful silence of a Barcelona Sunday morning—and being accosted by thieves who disappeared with the precious watch that had been on Ed's arm every day since his mother and I had given it to him decades before.

God and I had some serious discussions in the course of these episodes, and I did some serious whining. I didn't always handle these challenges gracefully. But to the extent I managed to retain either my manners or my zest for travel, I have Aunt Clyde to thank.

Everything's an adventure. Even the adventures we didn't actually want, with the limitations we didn't expect to face. Those are the times we grow the most. The lessons are clearer and the results last longer. I'm always making notes of things I could have done differently or better; journeys with sudden snafus give me plenty of items for the list.

Perfect travels—whether to far away places or the grocery store—offer few insights. It's the misadventures that bring us patience, faith, resourcefulness and, most importantly, the chance to pray to and rely on the God who created us.

When we can accept that, I'm sure that all of our journeys have the Lord's approval.

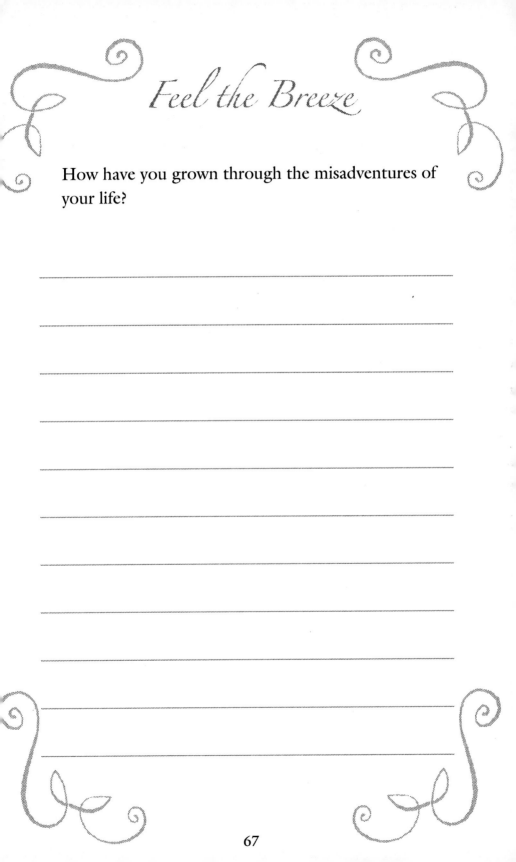

Feel the Breeze

How have you grown through the misadventures of your life?

THE GLOAMING

Day is dying in the West;
Heav'n is touching Earth with rest;
Wait and worship while the night
Sets her evening lamps alight
Through all the sky.

Holy, Holy, Holy Lord God of Hosts!
Heav'n and earth are full of Thee!
Heav'n and earth are praising Thee,
O Lord Most High!
—Mary A. Lathbury

DO YOU LOVE CERTAIN TIMES OF DAY MORE THAN OTHERS?

That first, bright glimpse of early morning? The wee hours of the night, when no one else in the world seems to be awake?

For me, that best-loved time is the gloaming.

"Gloaming" is an old-fashioned word barely used any more. It's that short time between sunset and dark when the light is slowly fading. It's a lovely, often quietly comforting, sometimes nostalgic few moments.

It's the time of fireflies.

I sat alone in the gloaming on my daughter's front porch in

Tennessee. Slowly I became aware of their presence: the little spots of yellow light that popped up here and there across her yard and the lawn across the quiet street. I felt as though they were angels, showing off their tiny beauty just for me.

As darkness crept in, the lights were less and less frequent. I waited. Just one more, I thought, just one more little light.

Suddenly, not two feet in front of my face—so close it startled me—the light blinked.

One more firefly hovered right there just for me. I think it was a spirit telling me goodnight.

Darkness settled down across the yards and the road. And God's presence filled the night.

Feel the Breeze

What time of day feels most soulful to you? Which of its sights and sounds speak most strongly of God's presence?

SECURITY QUESTION

My sheep listen to my voice; I know them and they follow me.
I give them eternal life, and they shall never perish;
no one can snatch them out of my hand.
—John 10:27-28

MY PHONE BEEPED. I HAD A TEXT. TWELVE-YEAR-OLD GRANDSON Jack had a question.

Where were you born?

Well, this is interesting, I thought.

Big Spring, Texas, I texted back.

His response: *Thanks.*

Why do you need to know that? I responded.

I'm trying to get into my DS and I can't. Mom set it up, so I tried Naples, FL but that didn't work. Yours didn't either.

Ah. The DS is some kind of electronic game device.

Well, I thought, isn't that interesting. In Jack's world, I've become the answer to a security question. I've reached a whole new level of identity.

That's the world we're living in now. Everything we do has a password or a code. None of the codes are supposed to be the same. If they are, the bad guys can access everything you've got.

Including your bank account. Which they do with relative ease anyway, it seems to me.

I don't know about your brain, but mine just can't remember all those different letters and numbers and symbols. Security questions are easier. You're likely to remember the name of your first dog sooner than you will some random string of nonsense. And of course, you'll know where you were born. You just have to remember whose birthplace you used when you set up the system. And which letters were upper case and lower case.

When I was 12 years old, all I had to know was my address and phone number. Now I don't dare forget where I keep information for all the important sites I visit in the cyber world. Humanity presses on to greater heights. And a lot of the time, "progress" feels like one step forward, two steps back.

But not always.

About a year before the DS question, Jack's mother called me one Sunday afternoon. "Mom," Lyn said, "do you have Skype on your computer?"

Well, no. Skype was one of those modern things for which I'd never really felt a need.

That changed in an instant. Ed and I had known that Jack was working on his decision to be baptized. We'd hoped we would have enough advance notice to be able to be there in person. It didn't work out that way. But Lyn explained that with Skype, Ed and I could watch Jack's baptism, which would take place that same evening.

I installed Skype in minutes with her long-distance help. At the appointed time, Ed and I sat in our house in Florida—but were also present at the lake near their church in Tennessee.

It was a beautiful, peaceful, twilight scene. With the church members gathered on the lake shore, Jack waded into the water with his dad and the youth pastor.

Then the pastor asked Jack the most important security question he will ever answer: "Do you love the Lord Jesus Christ and accept Him as your savior?"

With his affirmation, his father plunged Jack under the water.

Safe in the hands of Jesus! I don't mind telling you there were waterworks on this end of the scene!

Oh, the places we'll go. *That* security question will take us straight to heaven.

And the bad guys can't do a thing about it.

Feel the Breeze

Think about that all-important "security question" about accepting Jesus Christ as your savior. What memories or thoughts does it inspire for you?

NEW ACCESSORIES

Is not life more important than food,
and the body more important than clothes?
—Matthew 6:25

Who of you by worrying can add a single hour to his life?
—Matthew 6:27

MY LIFE TOOK AN UNEXPECTED TURN IN 2013. A DIAGNOSIS OF breast cancer was followed by a double mastectomy. Now I have new accessories: breast prostheses. Whether I choose to wear them at any given moment or not, they'll be part of my life forever.

Wigs were another accessory that my cancer brought me. I had them in blonde, auburn, brown and black. I was so careful to wear one or the other whenever I left the house. Occasionally, I covered my head with a hat—always something to cover up my chemo-ravaged scalp.

It wasn't a perfect solution. The first time grandson Nathaniel stayed overnight after I was good and bald, he headed for my bedside to wake me up. His mom, Becky, tried to stop him, but she didn't catch him in time. He was only four, but he was fast!

"Mimi," he whispered softly but urgently in my ear, "wake up. WHAT HAPPENED TO YOUR HAIR?!"

Even after he understood, he remained understandably curious. One day he asked me if my "underneath hair" was itching.

It was. Fiercely and without end.

Constantly scratching my head, I realized, wasn't much more attractive than the wisps of hair that were just beginning to grow by then. It was sort of like what had happened with my college friend Dori's clothes, a story I'll share later in this book. The wigs made me look better in the moment, but the "cover-up" of who I really was just didn't work.

Shortly after that, I decided I would rather be honest with myself and the world. I would wear what *I* had, not fake it with something else. I would remember that a smile is my most important accessory…worn with my own body and my own clothes.

Because trust in how God has created and re-created me isn't a bad accessory either.

Let me add that I'm not against trying to look better. I colored my hair for many years and continue to do so now that it's all grown back in. Since God gave me free will, I choose to be what another grandson, Andrew, once called, in puzzlement, a "brown haired granny."

And I still haven't learned the lesson of self-acceptance completely. There are days when finding that smile—and embracing the evolving appearance of my torso and scalp—is harder than others.

But I try to remember that I'm alive. Healthy again. Here to puzzle my grandchildren and savor God's world and spread God's word.

Is not life more important than food, and the body more important than clothes…and hair?

Feel the Breeze

Is there anything "itching" you these days—
something false, uncomfortable or inauthentic?

_____

_____

_____

_____

_____

_____

_____

_____

_____

_____

CHEERS, TEARS & CLOUDS OF WITNESS

Let us run with perseverance the race marked out for us.
—Hebrews 12:1

I AM A SUCKER FOR A GOOD DRAMATIC SPORTS STORY. TONIGHT I watched as the U.S. gymnastics team was selected for the Olympics in London. As they were snowed with red, white and blue confetti that stuck to the tears rolling down their cheeks, the proud young people—whose years of hard work had finally paid off— waved to the cheering crowd and hugged each other. I cried too.

Give me a golf tournament with a happy young champion like Bubba Watson winning The Masters and I'm a soggy mess when it's over. When my favorite NASCAR driver goes to Victory Lane, I'm right there cheering as they drench each other with whatever they're sponsoring today—Coke, beer, Mountain Dew.

Those who do their thing in the sports world work in front of a great many witnesses. Bubba Watson was surrounded that whole weekend by hordes of golf fans and sports media who recorded his every move as he marched from the first tee on Thursday to the 18th green on Sunday. Sometimes they were so close to him I wondered how he swung his club.

NASCAR drivers don fire suits and helmets and climb through

the window to settle into seats that are molded to their bodies. They drive their cars as fast as they'll go for miles and miles, and every move they make is crucial—whether they finish 1st or 43rd. They do it covered by the press and cheered by the fans in the seats and in the infield. The question from the media at the end is always the same: "Now, tell us how you feel!"

Cheers and celebration—that's what so much of life is all about. I recently pulled out the yearbook from our college days at the University of Florida. I wanted to show the kids a picture of their Mimi and PawPaw in our early days. And there we were... together...at the front of a pack of screaming, exulting Gator fans. We were welcoming our team home from a great win—the first time the Gators had beaten the Alabama Crimson Tide in a long, long time. Our eyes were half-shut, our mouths wide open, as the camera caught us in mid-scream. What a joyful memory!

The world of competitive sports mirrors life in so many ways. Giving your all, playing by the rules, learning how to lose and rejoicing in the victories are part of both, no matter how different sports and everyday existence seem.

My life has seen many celebrations and I'm thankful for each one of them. And they've been so varied. Birthdays, weddings, anniversaries, births, graduations, reunions, new businesses. You and I, as we live on this earth, travel from high point to high point. And if our eyes are on the right things, we find joys on the mountaintops and in the valleys. Don't you find that each season of life has its own celebrations? Even at a funeral, we can celebrate a loved one's life and character and smile at all the great memories.

One of my favorite parts of the Bible is Hebrews. Chapter 11 is the great By Faith chapter, where the writer recounts all examples recorded in Scripture of the early people of God who exhibited great faith and followed God in the face of great opposition. If we sit down and think about it, each of us could write our own By Faith story. Not our own faith journey, but the examples of faith shown to us by those whose lives have influenced us to believe.

Few of us will ever be called on to display strength, will and talent in dramatic competitions watched by hundreds, much less thousands, of fans. Our struggles will be quieter and more private.

Yet struggles we will have. And they will test us—our faith, our courage, our conscience.

But we will also have cheering sections…those who support us here on earth, and beyond. I love the encouraging vision of this offered in the first verse of Hebrews Chapter 12.

Therefore, since we are surrounded by such a great cloud of witnesses, let us throw off everything that hinders and the sin that so easily entangles. And let us run with perseverance the race marked out for us.

That great cloud of witnesses…they're up there cheering us on just like the fans at all those sporting events. "Come on! You can do it! Keep going! Don't give up! We'll be there at the finish line. We'll all be rejoicing with you!"

Next time you're "fighting the good fight," just think about all those souls who are cheering you on, just waiting to greet you when your race is done.

And we think cheers and celebrations in *this* life are exciting!

Feel the Breeze

Imagining your life as a great game, who do you envision cheering you on? How does their support help you persevere and celebrate?

TWO AGED QUILTS

Your word, O Lord, is eternal;
it stands firm in the heaven.
Your faithfulness continues
through all generations...
—Psalm 119:89-90

I SIGNED MYSELF IN ON THE VISITOR LOG OF THE NURSING home, slapped the sticky visitor label on my shirt, and went searching. Turning down the hallway next to Mama's room, I spotted them: two white-haired ladies in wheel chairs, both of them about 90 years old.

Anyone who didn't know would assume they were simply residents who had happened to meet in the facility. Their 60-year friendship wasn't visible as they sat together in the hall. But it was present, almost palpable.

My mother and Eunice—the two ladies—had become friends when I was a child. Eunice's daughter and I were in the same class in elementary school, lived in the same neighborhood, and attended the same church. And Herb, Eunice's husband, was a grove man like Daddy, which made a bond even more natural. Slowly, Mama and Daddy and Eunice and Herb formed one of those solid bonds of life that weathers the test of time.

As their kids grew up and their nests emptied, they shared restaurant meals and golf games. Once they had a little more money and time, they traveled together as well.

And then the men died.

Mama has Alzheimer's. She was no longer safe in her own home, so she moved to the nursing home first. Eunice followed a couple of years later. The first time I saw her in the facility, Eunice held my hands and laughed about the irony of it all.

"Your daddy and Herb used to talk about what your mother and I should do if anything ever happened to them," she said. "They told us we should get a house and live together. I don't think this is what they had in mind!"

"No, Eunice," I answered, "I'm sure it wasn't." *Still,* I added silently, *I think they'd be glad that you are both safe and well cared for.*

The saddest thing isn't that they are both old and infirm or that they are living in a nursing home. It's that Mama's Alzheimer's has wiped Eunice, Herb, and their shared past from memory. She remembers only my brother and me, and sometimes I'm not even sure about that.

Mama does seem aware that Eunice is somebody that she should know. Still, she makes no move to communicate. The most she does is to roll her wheelchair to Eunice's door and look in. She never crosses the threshold. Eunice seeks Mama out and attempts to talk to her, but Eunice is very soft-spoken and Mama is very deaf. Eunice doesn't hear well either, so even if my mother answered her, I guess the conversation would still be an exercise in futility.

Still, there is a bond there, laced together by more than 60 years of life. A connection, an undercurrent of feeling, there even though memories have failed, eyes have grown dim and ears have ceased to catch the sound waves. Watching them when they didn't know I was looking, I've seen Eunice reach over and rub Mama's arm. And though it's almost surely wishful thinking, I believe I see the slightest glimmer of warmth behind Mama's eyes.

As I left the nursing home that day, I had a fanciful thought. It struck me that the two women were like two old quilts. Made by the same sure hand, the quilts are faded and worn. In places the cloth is threadbare; in places a line of stitches is gone. But the pattern is still visible, and each quilt still echoes the design of the other.

The two quilts look right together, side by side in that nursing home hall.

Feel the Breeze

Who is woven into the fabric of your life, there even as the years pass?

_____

_____

_____

_____

_____

_____

_____

_____

_____

_____

ONE LIGHT, TWO LIGHTS, MANY LIGHTS

One of the ways we imitate God is by walking in the light.
When we become Christians, one of the metaphors that is used
to describe the difference in our life is that we now become
children of the light. Before, we were darkness itself.
—Thomas Kinkade and David Jeremiah, *The Secret of the Light*

BACK IN THE DAYS OF BENJAMIN FRANKLIN, THE WORLD WAS A pretty dark place once night fell.

His autobiography tells that Ben lived on a very dark street in Philadelphia. Indeed, most streets of his time were very dark. The danger of walking along and stepping into a hole or tripping over a rock or—worse yet—being grabbed in the darkness by a robber worried Ben.

Being a leader and a student of light, Ben tried an experiment. One night, he hung a lantern out by the street in front of his house.

Obviously, his neighbors noticed. The next night there were two lights. And then three or four.

Before long the entire street glowed with lanterns in front of each house.

What we do is remembered long after what we say…even when we do it right on our own doorstep.

Feel the Breeze

Remembering that it doesn't always take strenuous effort to spread the light, might you do something small today to help God's Word shine in the world?

_____

_____

_____

_____

_____

_____

_____

_____

_____

TRAINING WHEELS

For I am the LORD, your God, who takes hold of your right hand
and says to you, Do not fear; I will help you.
—Isaiah 41:13

"NO! IT DOESN'T HAVE TRAINING WHEELS!"

Granddaughter Charlotte recoiled from the bicycle like it was a snake about to strike. In a flash she ran behind the car parked in the driveway and hid so I couldn't see her.

When I got to her, the tears were running down her cheeks. "I'm scared. It doesn't have training wheels. I'll fall over," she wailed. We talked for a few minutes as I assured her I would help her. I would walk alongside and not let go. I would not let her fall. With my promise to hold onto the bike, Charlotte came around. We took off together. As she pedaled, I bent over, holding the bike by the back of the seat with one hand and the handle bar with the other while I trotted alongside.

We didn't have much time on this particular Sunday, so Charlotte didn't make a solo flight. But she will. Conquering her fear is a work in progress. The main thing she has to learn is that safety is but a step away, literally. For right now, there's me or a parent by her side. She'll learn soon enough that if she starts to fall, she simply has to put her feet on the ground.

I remember the day Daddy did that for me on the small road next to our fruit stand. And we have home movies of Daddy and Uncle Tom running back and forth on Atlantic Blvd in front of our house with Kenny as he mastered the art of balancing a two-wheeler.

Children naturally fear new experiences. We adults too pull back from unfamiliar territory, untested skills, and other leaps of faith.

Yet as the verse in Isaiah tells us, we need not fear; He will help us. We can count on his faithfulness and protection. Like a parent or grandparent trotting alongside a wobbling bike *and* like the solid ground under Charlotte's feet, He is always at our side.

Feel the Breeze

"Feet on the ground!" Are you trotting alongside someone, helping them move forward? Or are you yourself needing the security of those steady feet?

PEACE

He sends forth springs in the valleys;
they flow between the mountains...
—Psalms 104:10

IT WAS A GREAT BLESSING TO MY LIFE THAT I WAS ABLE TO GO to North Carolina to Girl Scout camp in my early teen years. I love the vision I hold in my heart of those twilight evenings sitting on the side of the hill overlooking the lake and singing. . My favorite song was "Peace I Ask of Thee Oh River." This was my first experience of being away from my family for an extended time. I was beginning to learn who I was and what was important to me. In those camp days, being immersed in God's serene beauty gave me peace; later, the memory became a mental "safe place to fall" in difficult times. Whenever I'm in the mountains, it comes back to me and reminds me that I am not alone.

This week, Ed and I have enjoyed the peace of sitting by a river. A few days of our own sandwiched between visiting grandchildren and a family wedding gave us time to seek out a quiet spot. We were thankful to find a small inn with porches and rocking chairs beside one of North Carolina's rippling rivers. Just the place to sit peacefully, enjoy the presence of God, and contemplate living serenely.

It's easy to find peace sitting by a river. But it's there for us even amid challenge and clamor. My memory helps quiet and calm me even when life is anything but peaceful. In moments of stress, in my heart I sing the song:

Peace I ask of thee, oh river
Peace, peace, peace
When I learn to live serenely
Cares will cease

From the hills I gather courage
Visions of the days to be
Strength to lead and faith to follow
All are given unto me.

Peace I ask of thee, oh river
Peace, peace, peace.

Feel the Breeze

Where or from what do you find peace? What helps you rediscover it in troubled times?

THE MOTHER OF THE BRIDE

On the third day a wedding took place at Cana in Galilee. Jesus's
mother was there, and Jesus and his disciples had also been invited
to the wedding. When the wine was gone, Jesus's mother said to him,
"They have no more wine."
"Dear woman, why do you involve me?" Jesus replied.
"My time has not yet come."
His mother said to the servants, "Do whatever he tells you."
—John 2:1-5

I MARRIED OFF TWO DAUGHTERS AND DID NOT SHED A TEAR AT either wedding. It wasn't that I didn't feel like crying. I did. I just didn't want to spend years to come looking at a bunch of pictures showing my blotchy face, swollen eyes and streaky makeup. So basically it was a vanity thing.

As I write this, it is summer and Ed and I are on the way to a family wedding. His cousin's only child—her daughter—is getting married. Of course it's a happy occasion, but for the bride's mom it's a tough time. In today's culture, the preparations leading up to a wedding are enough to turn any young woman and her mother into shrieking shrews. Shrews who, on the big day, are suddenly expected to be visions of family bliss posing angelically for pretty pictures. Well, miracles do happen.

"Please come and help me get through this!" my cousin begged. So I will do what I can to assist and console, because mothers understand these things. Just as Jesus's mother did.

My daughter Lyn was married in October 1995. Because she had been living in Tennessee for some time, she and David were married there. So there I was, planning my first wedding as the "MOB" and doing it long distance. And there were other challenges. They were being married in Knoxville, so we had to find a weekend when the University of Tennessee was playing football someplace else. It was hunting season, so we had to choose a time when the young pastor would not be in the woods hunting. In an amazing feat of logistics, the grace of a loving God and the help of a host of friends, we assembled all of our family and closest friends at the Radisson Hotel.

And so, on a chilly, rainy evening, Lyn and David were married at Wallace Memorial Baptist Church. One of the bridesmaids became ill at the absolute eleventh hour (5:00 p.m. for a 7:00 p.m. wedding) and had to be replaced. Because we certainly could not have an odd number of bridesmaids and groomsmen! I forgot that and other last-minute hiccups at the ceremony. It was beautiful, and I loved that Lyn wore my wedding dress. We all made it safely to the Radisson for a reception, where we got our first look at the wedding cake my daughter had ordered. It was beautiful and it was huge. We had cake for the masses for weeks.

My other daughter, Becky, and her "honey," Victor, were married in Vero Beach. That should have made things easier. HA! As I discovered, there is no "easier" when it comes to a wedding. That one was on the hottest afternoon of the year, a day in August 2001. It was not without its moment of bridesmaid drama. One of the girls dropped the top of her two-piece dress on her way to the church. She retraced her steps and it was found, lying on the floor at the hotel.

Becky is a singer, so naturally, the most important focus was the music. She assembled 11 singer friends and placed them in the balcony of First Baptist Church. They sounded like a choir of angels. My father raved about the music until his passing three months later. I am grateful to this day that he got to witness this ceremony before he died.

Since Lyn had worn my dress, Becky wore my wedding shoes. By the time Becky was married, Lyn and David had Andrew, who was four years old. Of course, he had to be part of the ceremony! He was so cute in his little tux with short pants and knee socks. He was less than thrilled but he did his best to do what we asked of him.

Every wedding has its own drama, highlights, catastrophes, hysteria. What helped me get through the ceremonies was a thought that came to me at Lyn's wedding. Right before I went down the aisle, I realized, *We have worked ourselves to death for this 30 minutes of time. I am not going to sit here and bawl and not be able to see it.* I can honestly say that when I got to the ceremonies, I was happy. By then I was on cruise control. Everything was in place. What would happen would happen. I didn't have to make any more decisions. Smile and make nice—that's all I had to do.

That, and appreciate God's grace.

Remember that wedding Jesus went to...where he turned the water into wine? He really did that, I'm sure, to keep the mother of the bride from having a meltdown. I get a kick out of the fact that it was his own mother who came to him and said "*Do* something." She was in a fixing mode—trying, obviously, to help out her friend. That's what mothers and their friends do.

It moves me that it was at a wedding that Jesus gave the world the first glimpse of his glory. In the midst of that happy setting, the one who came to save the world made sure nothing marred the occasion. That's the kind of savior he is.

Feel the Breeze

How has God been part of the treasured ceremonies of your life?

_____

_____

_____

_____

_____

_____

_____

_____

_____

_____

_____

TWO-SONG TOM

Hide me, O my Savior, hide,

Till the storm of life is past;

Safe into the haven guide,

O receive my soul at last.

—Charles Wesley, *Jesus, Lover of My Soul*

"JESUS, LOVER OF MY SOUL." WHENEVER I SEE THAT TITLE OR hear that hymn, I always think about my Uncle Tom.

Back in the late 1940s and 1950s, we took lots of car trips with Uncle Tom and my Aunt Clyde. The two of them plus Mama, Daddy, my brother Kenny and I would pile into whatever car was the newest and roomiest at the time and take off. I particularly treasure the memory of a summer trip to California: the six of us with a trunk full of luggage in a big boat of a car with no A/C, sailing across Texas, New Mexico, Arizona…with the windows open and the warm wind whipping through our hair.

As we drove along, Tom would periodically burst forth in song, an activity totally at odds with the rough "grove man" persona he adopted on ordinary days at home. He couldn't carry a tune to save his life, but on these road trips he sang lustily and loudly. He had two songs—"Bye Bye Blackbird" and "Jesus,

Lover of My Soul." Aunt Clyde would just cover her eyes with her hand and giggle.

As a kid, I wondered where he got these two completely different songs. Tom probably got "Bye Bye Blackbird" from the radio my father said they listened to. The source of the hymn was more mysterious. As an adult, he wasn't much of a church-goer, and I didn't think the hymn was something that really got his attention as he sat in the pew as a child.

As I recalled that long-ago memory the other day, the answer finally came to me. His mother. Uncle Tom heard the hymn from his mother. And she heard it from *her* mother. I remember many times hearing about his mother's beautiful voice. On summer evenings after she had fed her family, the family stories went, she would sit on the back steps of their big white frame house in Virginia and sing as darkness fell. I was told that her lovely voice would carry across the yard and the neighboring field to the delight of the neighbors. She also gave voice to the hymns she loved to sing at the little Methodist church nearby.

And so her grandson, my Uncle Tom, carried a few lines of a Charles Wesley hymn in his head because it had been sung to him by his grandmother and his mother. He may not have been an active churchgoer, but the faith was stuck in his soul.

That realization makes me very conscious of the things I've said and sung to my grandchildren. I recall a night several years ago when I was rocking the youngest one to sleep. He was about two years old at the time. I thought he was almost ready to be put down to sleep when he looked at me through slits of eyes and whispered, "Sing 'Jesus Loves Me.'" I sang and he slept and all was well with the world. I am confident that the song did more than merely lull him to sleep. We often pass down the faith through our songs and, I think, delight God in doing so.

As 3 John:4 puts it, "I have no greater joy than to hear that my children are walking in the truth."

It was a happy grandmother singing her "grand" to sleep with a hymn that night, just as it was a car full of happy people that rode across the country that summer. Thanks to Uncle Tom, we were serenaded along the way. Two-Song Tom..."Jesus, Lover of My Soul."

I'm sure his mama was sitting in heaven smiling.

Feel the Breeze

In songs, stories, writing, teaching, or some other manner unique to you: how do you pass on the lessons of your faith?

THE CROSS ON THE WATER

These commandments that I give you today are to be upon your
hearts. Impress them on your children. Talk about them when you sit
at home and when you walk along the road, when you lie down
and when you get up. Tie them as symbols on your hands
and bind them on your foreheads. Write them on the doorframes
of your houses and on your gates.
—Deuteronomy 6:6-9

Grace and peace to you from God our Father and the Lord Jesus
Christ; I thank my God every time I remember you.
—Philippians 1:2-3

MY GRANDMOTHER CARRIE SPENT SUMMERS IN NORTH CAR-
olina when I was a little girl. One evening, as we took a twilight
drive from Waynesville, she suggested we drive along the shores
of Lake Junaluska. She wanted to show me something special,
she said. The very words made *me* feel special too.

We soon reached the lake. There, cooled by the soft mountain
breezes, was a shining cross. It glowed with what seemed like an
unearthly light and seemed to be floating, as if by some miracle,
in the middle of the water. To say I was awed doesn't even come
close.

It was the cross at the Methodist Conference Center, but I'm not sure I understood that then. I am sure I didn't care. The whys and hows didn't matter, and Mema Carrie didn't trouble me with them. All that mattered was the cross, glowing and suspended over the still water.

Almost every evening we spent in Waynesville thereafter, viewing that cross was a must and a delight.

Much later in my life, I realized she wanted me to see that cross because her faith meant so much to her. Perhaps because she was not in good health, she realized she might not be with me always to tell me about it or about what it meant to her. So she gave me the best picture she could find: a lighted cross floating by God's grace in the middle of a timeless mountain lake.

What a simple, profound and magical way to pass on the faith.

Feel the Breeze

What sights make faith and God visible for you?
Could you share any of them with others?

CARVED COCONUT HEADS

Our mouths were filled with laughter,
our tongues with songs of joy.
—Psalm 126:2

For the Lord takes delight in his people...
—Psalm 149:4

THE SILLY-LOOKING COCONUT HANGING ON A PEG IN THE roadside shop immediately took me all the way back to my childhood. Ed and I were road-tripping and needing a break from the highway, so we pulled into a small fruit shop and got out to stretch our legs. As I headed to the restroom, there it was. A blast from my past. A coconut head pirate. Just the kind we sold at Kennedy Groves. I know God takes delight in his people because he gave us a sense of humor, joy in the world around us, the desire to make things as deliciously silly as carved coconut heads, and even the desire to buy them.

Our grove store wasn't unusual. Walk into any of the roadside fruit stands along US 1 in the 1950s and you would find pretty much the same assortment of merchandise. Oranges and grapefruit and their juice shared the spotlight with the tropical jellies made from exotic-sounding fruits like guavas. (Now there's an interesting little item that will deserve its own musing.) Candy always filled the shelves—everything from coconut patties to the much-beloved pecan logs. And who can forget the chocolate alligators? They helped send my brother and me to that Gator school in Gainesville!

You might also have seen a neat little device called the Citra Sipper. Somebody who was infinitely inventive came up with that one. We must have sold a bazillion of those things. It was a plastic tube you inserted into a piece of citrus fruit, making it possible to suck the juice straight from the fruit. The original, natural juice box!

As my mind scans the store, I see racks of serrated fruit spoons and knives, tables filled with bagged fruit and stacked high with boxes of candy, bins filled with bag-your-own fruit and the counter where the Yankees bellied up and soaked up all they could drink for ten cents. And there, hanging from a rack of giant hooks, is the weirdest thing of all.

As I said: God takes delight in his people. One of whom, picking up a coconut one day, thought, "What can I make out of this?" The result was one of the most garish creations to grace this planet. The mass of reddish-brown furry stuff inside the hard coconut shell became the hair for this monster, while stuck-on shells became ears. With carved out eyes, nose and mouth (the latter complete with ugly, gaping teeth) and a bright scarf for headgear, the thing became a coconut pirate. A loop atop the head allowed it to be hung on a rack, for sale to anyone willing to plunk down good money for this one-of-a-kind souvenir. What would the guys at the office say!

Surely these coconut creatures brought much fun and laughter when they reached their destinations. (Equally surely, some of that laughter came at the expense of the person who paid good money to bring such things home.) As I stood in that shop recollecting them, I wondered where they were now. Dark and dusty places all over this country...attics, closets, basements, thrift shops and, sadly enough, landfills...are home to those "funny things we brought back from that Florida vacation."

To which my brother and I—who got serious help toward an education from these silly things—can only say...Thank you, thank you.

Feel the Breeze

What silly object or small moment fills your mouth with laughter? Could you take a moment today just to relish the smile it gives you?

THE SUPER MOON

Then God said, "Let there be lights in the sky to separate day from night. These lights will be used for signs, seasons, days, and years. They will be in the sky to give light to the earth." And it happened.

So God made the two large lights. He made the brighter light to rule the day and made the smaller light to rule the night. He also made the stars. God put all these in the sky to shine on the earth, to rule over the day and over the night, and to separate the light from the darkness. God saw that all these things were good. Evening passed, and morning came. This was the fourth day.
—Genesis 1:14-19 MSG

I LEARNED ABOUT A LOT OF THINGS IN THE SUMMER OF 2013, when I was diagnosed with breast cancer. I learned about cancer, about chemotherapy, the effect on the body of white blood cells or the lack thereof, the absolute necessity of hydration. I learned that all of these things together can change the strong, energetic body I'd always taken for granted into a fragile shell.

The lesson began at my oncologist's office. When the sweet lab technician there looked at me and saw the results of my blood test, she spoke without hesitation. "Oh, you're going to the hospital," she said in her softly sweet, caring tone.

Under any other circumstance, I likely would have argued. This time, I was too sick to care. My only thought was: *How fast can I get to a hospital bed and lie down?*

For the next two days, all I could do was lie in that bed. Breathe, eat a bit of food, sleep, breathe, sleep again: that was my routine. The sleep part of it came on often and suddenly, teaching me that it makes doctors very nervous when you go to sleep while they're talking to you. It would have been funny if I'd had the energy to laugh.

I couldn't manage even the most minor things. Noticing that everyone who visited wore a mask, I remember thinking, "Gosh, am I contagious?" But it felt like too much effort to ask. I finally got up the energy to ask the question. It was startling to know the masks weren't to protect them from me, they were to protect me from them! Suddenly I understood fully why we need all those white blood cells.

By the third day, thanks to continuous rest and all of the stuff that was pumping through the IV in my arm, I was enjoying a significant rally. A shower never felt so good; food was actually appealing again. By late afternoon that day, I was able to walk down the hall. Instead of getting back in bed, I sat in the comfortable chair by the window—not a big change, but a significant one. That was another sign of my healing: the bed that had beckoned like Heaven three days before now had no appeal.

From my fourth floor room, which faced the east, I could see to the Indian River and beyond. My room was quiet. Peace settled over the landscape as I watched the twilight cover the earth. Lights began to twinkle here and there across the evening sky.

In awe of the peaceful sight, I experienced a quiet in my spirit like none I've ever known. My thoughts went no further than that moment. I focused on serenity and rest and the enjoyment of being alive.

I must have dozed for a few minutes. When I roused, darkness had fallen fully. Suddenly, something in the night caught my eye. I turned, looked, and nearly fell out of my chair.

It was the Super Moon—a full moon at its closest approach to Earth. The biggest moon I've ever seen was rising right before my eyes, immense and golden, as if it was coming up out of the river. I felt like I could reach out and put my hand on its face.

I sat there for at least two hours watching the moon inch its way up the darkening sky, growing smaller as it went higher. Somehow, the higher it went, the brighter it got.

What a sight! It was utterly extraordinary. Yet the moon does the same things, in some form or other, every night without fail.

Sitting in that chair, even knowing that my fight with a serious disease was by no means over, I thanked God.

For the splendor of the Super Moon, a quiet evening, and a hospital chair from which to watch it rise.

And for the reassurance that God is God and will be here no matter what.

On the fourth day, He gave us His light in two forms: one to rule over the day and one to rule over the night.

In giving us constant light, even when our eyes see mostly darkness, he gave us the sign that He is always with us.

Encouraging, inspiring moments with God are often tucked into tough times. Life's hard experiences make us feel our need for Him, and our need is answered. If we look around us, there will always be a sign that we're not forgotten. It may not be a signal like the Super Moon: startling, splendid, once-in-a-lifetime. But even if it is only an ordinary moon, a fragile crescent barely visible in the night sky, it tells us that His grace and mercy and encouragement is there beside us.

No wonder, after giving us light on the fourth day, God saw that it was good.

For me, it was evening, then it was morning, then the doctor sent me home. I carried the blessing of God's moon with me.

Feel the Breeze

How does God signal his presence in your dark times? How have you been reminded that He is always there?

Fall

BORROWED CLOTHES

And why do you worry about clothes? See how the lilies of the field
grow. They do not labor or spin. Yet I tell you that not even Solomon
in all his splendor was dressed like one of these.
—Matthew 6:28-29

AH, VANITY! THY NAME IS COLLEGE COED, CIRCA 1960s. I WAS
once one of those young ladies. It's surprising how much "her"
thoughts and actions—and the lessons learned then—speak to
me still, all these years later.

Flash back to 1963: the dating years. Ed and I had been going
together since September. It was now two months later. The
relationship was serious and steady…very steady. Friday night was
coming. The most pressing question was: what would I wear? It
had to be something new and different. Forget the Humanities
test and the English paper. The subject of the hour was clothes!

This was a rare moment in my life. Living in the dorm room
next door to me was a girl, Dori, who was about my size. Not
many girls were as tall and lanky as I was. Unlike me, Dori cared
absolutely nothing for clothes. She wore the same three things
over and over wherever she was going. Her mother, however,
cared a lot about how she looked and sent her boxes of beautiful,
expensive clothes regularly. While her friends watched, me

included, with our palms getting sweaty and our tongues drooling, Dori hastily unpacked the boxes, put the clothes away…and ignored them.

"Wear them! Use them! I don't care!" she would say to me.

I resisted this urging until a particular Friday afternoon. Ed and I were going to the movies. That meant walking 13 blocks from campus to theater in the cold. I needed something that was just right to wear. Dori was out but she never locked her door. I remembered her urging to borrow anything I wanted.

In a moment I was standing in front of her bountiful closet—I had seen her take the outfit out of the box just days before. Soft purple and lime green plaid wool pants—lined, of course—and a soft wool purple crewneck sweater to match. I scurried back to my room and ripped off my boring old clothes.

She was right. Her clothes fit me perfectly. The outfit was exactly what I needed for my evening out. I left her a note of exuberant thanks—I have manners, you know—and headed downstairs.

Ed and I walked arm in arm, hand in hand, chatting all the way like all the other couples on the sidewalks of Gainesville that night. I recall no other details of the early part of the evening. The fun started on the walk back.

It started to drizzle early in our trek. We hugged closer as he raised the umbrella he had wisely brought. But then…cloudburst. Monsoon. Drenching downpour.

The umbrella was no match for it. Wind whipped the water sideways and even upwards. There was no place to get inside out of the deluge. We simply ran.

Had I been in my own clothes, it wouldn't have mattered. But in these clothes, it mattered a lot. Suddenly I realized that strange things were happening to the pants. Wool, I learned that night, doesn't always maintain its shape when it gets sopping wet.

When at last we reached the dorm, we said a hasty goodnight. I signed myself back in and climbed the stairs to the fourth floor. Every step left a puddle. I opened the door and looked toward the other end of the hall where I lived. Dori was standing in front of her room. At the sight of me, she fell to her knees in laughter. By the time I got to the middle of the hall, I too was laughing so hard I could hardly walk.

The sweater, now a mass of matted wool, had stretched to mid-thigh. The pants were even more pitiful. One leg had shrunk to the bottom of my calf, with the lime green lining hanging out and rubbing the back of my shoe. The other leg had stretched so long I was dragging it. Behind me a wet trail like a giant snail's was following me.

I never touched her clothes again. Or anyone else's, for that matter.

Now why would that memory speak to me here in my later life? Because it's a gentle and funny lesson in self-acceptance.

I learned that night that other people's clothes—like other people's beliefs, opinions, lifestyles, habits—may seem to fit us for a while. They may even seem to make us more attractive, or more successful, than we really believe we are. But we can never truly sustain the deception they create. Whether the truth of who we are is revealed in a funny way or a painful one, we are ultimately revealed as our true selves.

The lilies of the field do not labor or spin.

They don't try to be roses or daises or cherry blossoms, either.

Feel the Breeze

How has God helped you remember to be true to who and what you are?

_____

_____

_____

_____

_____

_____

_____

_____

_____

_____

_____

LEARNING FROM DADDY

Blessed is the man who fears the Lord,
who finds great delight in his commands.
—Psalm 112:1

I LEARNED A LOT FROM MY FATHER—MY DADDY, AS I THINK OF him. If you're not a Southerner like I am, that may sound rather childlike. But we use the term "daddy" forever, even when we're 70 and our father is 95.

Daddy taught me to love sports. To pay attention while watching them. To throw a football well. To drive—even though the lesson was completed by the high school's Drivers Ed program once I'd plowed the family car into a parked truck. To work hard. To do things right. All of these lessons, among many others he taught me, are ingrained in my soul.

But his most important lessons he taught me were about honoring God. And he shared them without saying a word.

On Sunday morning, he taught me, you go to church. Left side of the sanctuary, close to the back. Read your bulletin, use your hymnal, pay attention. Sit still. (He had a real thing about sitting still.) Don't chew gum. Don't go to sleep. And for heaven's sake, don't talk! Yes, those instructions were spoken. But the deeper message was what he did: brought us to church every

Sunday, rain or shine, healthy or sick, no matter what.

Another thing he taught by example: My father prayed. Most of the time it was after we had all gone to sleep—I know about it mostly from childhood wanderings out of bed. He would go into the darkened living room, to the far end of the couch, and onto his knees. We never talked about it; it was just something he did. Though he never discussed his prayer life, I know that's what got him through the many challenges of raising a family and owning a business to provide for them. As a child, I didn't understand the deep meanings of a tired businessman and father making the time to pray on his knees every night. But once I'd seen it, it was a model I didn't forget.

Last but very much not least, my daddy taught me that the Lord was always there. God seemed always present for him. He often sang to himself, usually the old hymns of the church. One of his favorites was "I Love to Tell the Story." In his later years, he would sit in his recliner, stare off into space and sing himself a hymn. It was as if he was looking at those "unseen things above," seeing things most of us are too rushed or distracted to see.

Daddy was no saint. He could be a profoundly ornery, cantankerous person. Yet reverence for God was woven throughout everything he did, from his hardest work to his most relaxed play.

I got so much from what Daddy said.

But I learned far more from what he *did*.

Feel the Breeze

Whose example taught you to live in God's presence? How does that example inspire and guide you?

PORCHES AND ROCKING CHAIRS

Be still...and know that I am God.
—Psalm 46:10

I THINK EVERYBODY IN THE WORLD NEEDS A PORCH AND A rocking chair. Maybe it should be a law that we all have to sit down for at least 30 minutes a day and just be quiet. Just sit and rock and look at God's world and let Him talk to us.

Ed and I are spending a few days in a cabin in the North Georgia mountains. The best thing about the whole place is the porch and the comfy rockers. We rock, we talk, we read, we just sit. After a busy week herding two energetic little boys, the quiet regimen is just what we need. The porch is completely surrounded by tall shade trees. Here and there, a squirrel hangs by his back legs to pull his dinner from surrounding branches. As evening comes on, crickets fill the woods with their unique, gentle symphony.

Our world has grown so noisy: music in elevators and restaurants, TV in doctors' offices and banks, the ever-present sound of cell phones. We can barely hear ourselves think, much less discern the voice of the Creator.

Here, in the stillness and near silence, I can hear God's voice.

Sometimes his words drift into my mind as snippets of Scripture or hymn. Sometimes it is a wordless communication, as subtle and meaningful as the soft breezes that occasionally rustle the leaves beyond the porch. His peace, his comfort, his wisdom fill me as I sit rocking.

We'll never truly hear God talking unless we can quiet our own man-made clamor. And we have to do that individually... one at a time...in each heart.

Take my advice. Find a porch. Put a comfortable rocking chair on it. Sit down and be quiet. You might be surprised what you hear.

Feel the Breeze

Have you allowed yourself to simply sit, be still, and enjoy listening to the silence lately? If not, how might you find time for such a moment?

ACTION HEROES

*Then some Jews came from Antioch and Iconium and won the crowd
over. They stoned Paul and dragged him outside the city, thinking he
was dead. But after the disciples had gathered around him, he got up
and went back into the city.*

—Acts 14:19-20 MSG

*When I was a boy, I always saw myself as a hero in comic books and in
movies. I grew up believing this dream.*

—Elvis Presley

"Mimi, you gotta watch me!" Jack was pushing his bike
as he begged for my attention. He didn't have to beg. He had
me with "Mimi." We were in the garage underneath their East
Tennessee home. The slope up to the street is steep but his strong
ten-year-old legs pushed the bike up to the road. He turned
around to face the challenge he saw in his mind and stood there
like Rambo ready to attack. I had my cell phone camera clicked
to video to capture this auspicious moment and save it for all
posterity.

"OK, Mimi!" he yelled as he threw his leg over the bike and
stood up on the pedals. I knew he had done this before but I
prayed I wasn't about to record a disaster. I caught my breath as

he pointed the bike down and started pedaling as hard as he could. He flew down the driveway and expertly maneuvered between the two Bradford pear trees at the bottom. Like the action hero of the world, he swooshed in an arc at the foot of the drive and stopped with a flourish. Both arms shot into the air in a signal of triumph.

"Great, Jack!" I gave him the phone so he could view his performance.

"I'm going again!" And he was off to the street for an encore. I think we had about three encores that day.

I love this quote from Elvis for Jack because I'm sure Jack has an action hero for an alter ego. Most likely it's one of those Transformer things or something like that. Even though he loves the outdoors, he's a crackerjack video-game player. He also loves music. He can be seen most Sundays in the congregation of the contemporary worship church playing air guitar keeping perfect time with the music…music that extols the greatest Action Hero there will ever be.

When it comes to action heroes, Jesus is—of course—the leader of the pack. But let's not overlook his early followers…the ones who received power when the Holy Spirit came on them and they became his witnesses. (Acts 1:8) It's because these brave people, like Peter and Paul and so many others, took the stoning and all the other persecution that we have the salvation message today. The message of Jesus's crucifixion and resurrection gave them a dream and a hope not just for themselves but for all of us who believe. That hope is eternal life.

The young boy Elvis was dreaming big dreams for his future. Amazing how that turned out! Dreams are the stuff that push us along the road of life. I don't know what dreams are blowing around in Jack's head. What will he do? Where will he go? All I know right now is that his parents are giving him a solid Christian upbringing. And I know that even though I don't know what it is—and he doesn't either at this point—God has a plan for his life and He is already there in Jack's future. What kind of action hero will he be? I hope I have the privilege to see at least some of it.

Feel the Breeze

What dreams and prayers do you have for those who follow you?

_____

_____

_____

_____

_____

_____

_____

_____

_____

POINT A TO POINT A

The Lord said to him, "Go back the way you came..."
—1 Kings 19:15

ELIJAH HAD A GREAT ADVENTURE BEFORE HEARING THE WORDS above from God. He spent time in the desert where he was fed by ravens. He challenged the prophets of Baal and asked God to send the fire to burn up the sacrificial oxen. When God burned up everything, Elijah ordered all the prophets of Baal to be slaughtered. Naturally, that made Queen Jezebel angry; she let him know, to use modern phrasing, that he was a dead man. Nothing to do but hide in the desert to wait for the rain that he had promised the people would come. The rain finally came, pouring out of an almost clear sky.

And God said to Elijah "Go back the way you came." Elijah's best way forward...was back.

His way back was difficult and dangerous. He was returning to Damascus to find his successor, Elisha; his mission was sacred and his life was on the line.

Sometimes, God's direction is like that voice on the GPS: "Recalculating! Do a legal u-turn!" We may not have been going in the right direction. We may have passed our destination some time before. We may not have been clear about where we were going. The only thing we can do is turn around and retrace our steps…no matter how frustrating, time-consuming or just plain impractical that seems.

I'm always reminded of this lesson when I recall an episode from a trip to Italy Ed and I made in 2010. It was the trip of a lifetime in more ways than one.

Our first stop was the seaside town of Stresa, on the shores of Lake Maggiore. The lake, with its backdrop of the Swiss Alps, is postcard gorgeous. One day we took an excursion along the lake road into Switzerland. Need I say it was a beautiful hour? Ed drove our small rental car at a leisurely pace. Before long we breezed into the next country.

The next country. Where, we quickly learned, the Euros in our pockets did not work. Switzerland remains on the Swiss franc. (Note to self: Do your homework.) Without finding a bank, we couldn't put money in the parking meter, let alone treat ourselves to lunch.

Forget it, we agreed. There were plenty of nice places back across the border where our money *would* work.

Go back the way we came. That's what we wanted to do. However, it was more difficult than it sounds. First we had to deal with the one-way street we were on, then with the heavy flow of traffic. Before we knew it, we had driven straight into the mouth of a tunnel that went we knew not where. There was no chance to pull off the road to consult a map or ask directions. Just drive. And drive and drive. Fast.

It was a nerve-wracking drive. I tried to remember my Aunt Clyde's mantra, "Everything's an adventure," but it was difficult. We had no idea where this long, long tunnel would dump us out. We adventured in it for at least 25 minutes. *What do we do when we get to the end?* we asked each other. *If we don't know where we are, how can we know where to go?*

Ed finally began to realize we were going to have to retrace our course, which meant going back through that tunnel.

So, moments after we emerged into the daylight, we had turned back into the tunnel. Just as before, it was dark, it was fast, it was long. We drove in silence. What else was there to say? Half an hour later, we were back where we started from: still lost, but able to find our way back over the Swiss border. Within the hour, we were lunching at a lakefront restaurant that was only too happy to accept our currency. In the sunshine and with good food in front of us, we realized that it was, of course, funny rather than frightening: exactly the kind of adventure Aunt Clyde was speaking of.

Unlike Elijah's, ours was a purely secular, even silly, experience. But though it speaks on a different level, it makes a similar point.

Sometimes, we're all lost. It's tempting to try to go forward… especially in our culture that values speed, achievement, efficiency. But sometimes, the best way to rediscover the right path is to go from Point A…right back to Point A.

I try to remember both Elijah and that tunnel when I feel driven to push on at full speed even when I'm not sure where God wants me to go.

Feel the Breeze

Is there something you feel lost in now? What would happen if you retraced some of your steps?

_____

_____

_____

_____

_____

_____

_____

_____

_____

TRAIN UP A CHILD

I have no greater joy than to hear that my children
are walking in the truth.
— 3 John:1:4

CHARLOTTE WAS ABOUT THREE YEARS OLD WHEN SHE STOPPED us in our tracks one evening.

Ed and I were headed out for dinner with Charlotte and her parents during a visit to Jacksonville, Florida. The five of us were packed into the car, waiting for a traffic light to change. The turn took us due west, straight into the sight of a brilliant sunset. The magnificence of God's creation literally filled the car with golden light.

Charlotte expressed the joy for all of us: "Look what Jesus made for me!"

How affirming—how uplifting!—to know that this three-year-old already thought of Jesus in personal terms.

Fast forward nearly five years. One night, Charlotte wrote God a letter and asked Him a question. Leaving it by her bed, she expected a written answer, like the ones she got from Santa Claus or his Elf on the Shelf, Jingle. In the ensuing conversation with her mother, she learned that God doesn't talk to us that way. God speaks through his Word and our hearts. As the conversation ended, she prayed and asked Jesus into her heart. The ministers at her church talked with her and two weeks later, she was baptized.

I'm so glad my daughter took Charlotte's letter seriously. It's easy to miss the significance of such moments in the rush of life. But they are opportunities for both the child and we ourselves to grow closer to God. Even as little children, we come to Jesus with as much knowledge as we have and grow as long as we live.

Ed and I shared in the experience of Charlotte being baptized into the faith. It was another visit to Jacksonville. We were there at Deermeadows Baptist Church that Sunday morning to witness her immersion. What a joy it is to know that our grandchildren are being led by Christian parents and nurtured by their churches.

The most meaningful part of the service came when Charlotte was standing with the pastor in the pool. He asked everyone in the congregation who knew her or had taught her in a class to stand. So many people stood up!

"Look, Charlotte," he said, "all of these people are here to help you along your way on your Christian walk. You are not alone here."

We have been blessed to see three of our four grandchildren make their professions of faith and be baptized. Our oldest grandsons live in Tennessee. Andrew, the oldest, entered the pool on an Easter Sunday. We were there. Jack, his brother, was baptized in a lake, That one came about so quickly that we had to enjoy it through the magic of Skype.

Charlotte's brother, Nathaniel, is four. We have one more to bring into the fold! He's already following what his parents value. He told his father earnestly, "I want Jesus in my heart! I want to be baptized!" And of course, he wants to follow what his sister does. He is impressed that she has been baptized. He loves it when she reads to him and many of the books she reads are Christian books. She can lead her brother along the same path of truth.

Even a child can help train up a child.

Feel the Breeze

When have you shared the blessing of witnessing a child's path as he or she begins following God? How do the memories touch and enrich you?

THE PRODIGAL DAUGHTER

Simon, stay on your toes. Satan has tried his best to separate all of you from me, like chaff from wheat. Simon, I've prayed for you in particular that you not give in or give out. When you have come through the time of testing, turn to your companions and give them a fresh start.
—Luke 22:31-32 MSG

"My son," the father said, "you are always with me, and everything I have is yours. But we had to celebrate and be glad, because this brother of yours was dead and is alive again; he was lost and is found."
Luke 15:31-32 MSG

IT WAS DEFINITELY A FAITH BREEZE MOMENT. AS I LOOKED around at the scene, I felt God say in my spirit, "I told you she would be okay."

Lyn was sitting at the table in her kitchen. She looked so pretty with her makeup and hair all done, ready for the day. The kitchen was cleaned up, the breakfast dishes put away. The devotion book and Bible she had read earlier were stacked neatly on the table. Just to finish the tableau, her little pug climbed up into her lap. I had to take a picture. And thank God for his faithfulness and protection.

We went through a time of testing, of being shaken and sifted like wheat, when Lyn was in high school and college. Lyn tested every rule we made. She was always looking for the party. She seemed to be trying to walk just as close as she could to the boundary between right and wrong without falling permanently into the "wrong" side.

Satan was having a field day with us. I'd love to tell you we handled things like one of those perfect TV families, but what a whopper of a lie that would be. We were all in tumult, and the situation did divide us, at least temporarily. Ed and I fought each other about what we should do to deal with the situation. Becky fought us and her sister because she was graduating from high school and going to college and our focus was so divided. Lyn fought all of us because she wanted to be left alone to live her life as she chose. There was depression, there was deep hurt, there was embarrassment. We yelled, we cried, we hugged, we prayed. It seemed to be the nightmare that wouldn't end.

The first verse from Luke I quoted above became my safe place to fall during those years. I had the assurance that Jesus himself was praying for me—for all of us—that we would not give in and give out. I had the assurance that our faith would not fail. I had the assurance that when it was all over, we could use the testimony to strengthen those around us and to give them a fresh start.

But then…Lyn went to college. She left college. She worked various jobs. And finally—slowly—realization came.

Through the doors of community college, she got back into the school she had started with. Eleven years after beginning, she graduated with a bachelor's degree. By this time, she was married to a lovely man and had given birth to a wonderful son. In the midst of her family responsibilities, she went on with her hard-won education. She now holds a master's degree.

Lyn told me once that she wouldn't change anything about her life, because everything she has been through has made her what she is today. That, my friends, is maturity.

During Lyn's difficult years, another text from Luke that I relied on was the story of the Prodigal Son. I read and re-read it until I knew it by heart. There is such wisdom there. I saw that the prodigal son had to reach his own "bottom," as 12-step programs say. I saw that he and only he knew where that was. I saw that his family was powerless.

And I saw that there was a promise of return. I just didn't know if it would be in this life or the next.

During these years, our youth pastor reminded me that we had raised Lyn with faith in God. Now, we had to trust it. I hung on to that thought. "Lord, she knows you," I prayed more than once. "Please protect her. Keep her safe."

To see my daughter as she is today is a statement of faith to the world that we can begin again.

It is a profound gift to her father, her sister, and her own young family. And it is a profound gift to me. Her wisdom, her strength, and her inner beauty today are worth every bit of earlier pain. I am grateful for her transformation, and just as grateful for the lessons I myself learned at her side.

Those who have never experienced the pain of the prodigal will never know the joy of the return.

Feel the Breeze

When you are powerless to help someone struggling, how might remembering God's many promises of return and healing help ease your fears?

_____

_____

_____

_____

_____

_____

_____

_____

_____

_____

HONORING THE FAMILY

Honor your father and your mother, so that you may live long in the
land the Lord your God is giving you.
—Exodus 20:12

MY MOTHER RECENTLY ASKED ME TO SHARE SOME FAMILY memories. I remember my Nannie, of course, because we were with her if we weren't with Mom. Her relentless energy and ability to do anything was amazing. We pushed that woman but she would never relent. We only got our way when she allowed it with a little grin of "Ok, you got me but I let you!"

We were always cared for and enjoyed our time because she wanted us to have fun. She taught us to fish and always had a closet for our toys. She let us dress up and put on plays. She endured our radio station and made us food whenever we wanted. She had a pool and made sure we spent a lot of time in the pool and in the sun. We spent a lot of time with her in the summer. She would tell us we better get out there and enjoy the pool,

---

This essay is shared by my daughter, Lyn Foster. As I said of her sister, Becky's, piece in this book, which appears on page 173, I am touched and honored by the wisdom and faith of my grown-up girls.

143

because we would hate it when we had to be back in that old schoolhouse (with air conditioning!).

Our entertainment on Saturday nights with her and Grandpa was watching *Lawrence Welk* and *HeeHaw*. We could go to Disney at a moment's notice and run them all over the park. Unfortunately, (because both Nannie and Grandpa were "germophobic") we couldn't ever use the public toilet in a roadside gas station. It was a long trip between Vero Beach and Orlando, so we had to learn how to "go" in the tall Florida grass on the side of the road!

The memories I have of their house, and our whole family all together, make me very happy. We were a single unit growing and living life. Living so close together, we were able to gather for the Sunday meal almost every week. Of course, that Sunday meal always followed church.

My sister Becky and I never had to be alone because we always had close family to be with, and it was good. It still is good today.

The closeness we had in that family unit gave me a model for raising my own family. And it gave Becky and me a glimpse of what God's love is like.

Feel the Breeze

What "ordinary," everyday family times have influenced your own life, and the lives of your children if any?

_____

_____

_____

_____

_____

_____

_____

_____

_____

_____

JUST KEEP WALKING

*I press on toward the goal to win the prize for which God
has called me heavenward in Christ Jesus.*
—Philippians 3:14

I THOUGHT HE WOULD GET A TAXI.

We were dressed in our business clothes, my brother and I. Him in his suit and tie. Me in my jacket dress, hose and heels. Yes, hose. This was back in the '80s when well-dressed women still wore those awful things. And, of course, the heels that—in my small town perception—were required to stroll the sophisticated streets of New York if you wanted to look sharp.

We were headed to one of the major radio stations in the City to advertise our family company's mail order gift fruit. It was November, the beginning of the all-important holiday gift season. One of the perks of working in this family business was the chance to make these trips and spend time with my brother. Promoting the business was our job and we enjoyed doing it together. This was my first visit to the New York stations. Had it been my second, the shoes would surely have been different!

We stepped out the door of the hotel to the busy din of a normal New York morning. People walking full speed crammed the sidewalks. Cars, busses and taxis jerked their way through the get-to-work traffic, blowing their horns as if the noise would somehow move things along. I looked at the taxis with hope. But the brother had different ideas.

"It's not far," he said. "We can walk faster than a taxi could drive us there."

I couldn't argue with him. The scores of yellow taxis weren't moving any faster than the rest of the traffic. All of the vehicles except a few messengers on bicycles were just inching along.

So my brother headed off. Uptown or downtown, I never knew which. It didn't matter. Just follow that grey suit and walk, I told myself. In those stupid shoes.

Periodically, we would have to stop on a street corner to wait for a traffic light to change. At each one, the rivulets of sweat coursing down my cheeks and underneath my clothes grew wider and deeper.

"How much further?" I asked.

"Oh, not far. We're almost there. Just keep walking." Easy for him to say.

When at last we reached the building that housed the station, I asked for the nearest ladies' room. There, I mopped myself up. Laying paper towels on my face, I dried my wet cheeks. So much for my carefully applied makeup, which was now on the towels. I could do nothing for the parts of me below my face. My body would just have to dry on its own. I hoped my deodorant and perfume didn't fail me. As for my feet, they had been numb for blocks.

I pulled myself up straight, put a smile on my face and emerged, hobbling. Brother was standing there grinning. "Ya okay?"

"Just great. No problem."

We entered the office of the radio station right at our appointed time, smiling and looking calm, cool and collected.

All because we just kept walking.

Life is like that. A challenge appears before us. Distance needs to be covered. It looks like a long way. No matter. We cover it one step at a time. The challenge changes, but the process is always the same. Make the commitment. One thing at a time.

Building a house? One board, one brick at a time.

Writing a song? One note at a time.

Packing fruit? One orange at a time.

Writing a book? One word, one paragraph, one page at a time.

I've been writing this book for a long time now. The longer I've pressed on, the more I've craved the prize of the finished product. But completion didn't come from "thinking big." It came together when I focused on one thing at a time. Word by word, line by line, essay by essay. *Just keep going,* I reminded myself. Even if any given moment along the way wasn't pretty.

Like walking through New York with my brother, we get where we're going when we just commit to keep walking.

The Apostle Paul, along with his followers, carried the Gospel message to the world after the resurrection of Jesus. Their story is told in the Book of Acts. They were so committed to giving that hope of eternal life to everyone who would listen that they walked from town to town, preaching in the synagogues, in the streets and in the homes of those who were desperate to hear. For the sake of that Gospel, they endured hardship and persecution the likes of which we can only imagine. A sweaty morning on the streets of New York is nothing by comparison. They had a mission and a message. And they accomplished God's work by pressing on toward the Ultimate Prize....

One. Step. At. A. Time.

Feel the Breeze

Are you walking through a challenge today? Can you manage one more step, asking God for the strength to just keep walking?

PUT ON THE GRITS!

But you are a shield around me, O Lord;
you bestow glory on me and lift up my head.
—Psalm 3:3

Few people in Indian River County would recognize the name Carrie Kennedy. They might know her sons, Thomas and Purnell. But the lady who lived most of her life in the white frame house on the road that led down to the river passed this way leaving few footprints in the Florida sand.

To me, she was Mema Carrie, and she was unforgettable—nothing short of amazing. She was a Florida pioneer because she had to be.

It was about 1910 when she and her brother traveled to Florida from their birthplace on Virginia's Eastern Shore, a spit of land between the Chesapeake Bay and the Atlantic Ocean. The climate there was making her sick— the doctors told her parents when she was a young teenager that if she didn't get to a better climate, she likely would not survive to adulthood.

So her family arranged for her to live with an uncle in Florida. Florida at that time was mostly sandspurs, palmettos and mosquitoes, but its climate would be a bit kinder to her asthma. The fact that she lived 65 years would have amazed those doctors.

And not only did she live, she married my grandfather and gave birth to six children, five of whom survived to lead full adult lives.

A vision of what must have been the saddest, most difficult time in her life came to me as I read the cold hard facts of her life on a genealogy chart. Comparing the dates of the births of her babies and then noting the death date of her one child that died, I realized that she had given birth to a daughter just about six weeks prior to the death of Johnny, her firstborn. Imagine dealing with the demands and discomforts of recovering from birth and nursing a newborn, caring for another healthy toddler, and mothering a sick little boy in his final days. The clash of emotions between joy and grief must have been unbearable. How do you deal with such emotional highs and lows when your own health is so fragile?

On her birthday in 1929, as the horror of the Great Depression began to grip the country, her husband died. She was left with five offspring ranging in age from 14 down to to 7. They had the house they lived in, 20 acres of grapefruit and the fish in the nearby Indian River. Her oldest son, Thomas, quit school at 14 to support the family.

I'm told that whenever there was a crisis, her first response was to start a pot of grits cooking on the stove. Whatever was happening, her family would need to eat. Those grits were a staple in her household and a symbol of the practicality with which she approached life. They accompanied the many pans of fish her sons brought home from the river.

The family's very survival depended on those fish. The tale goes that when the boys reached a certain spot on the road, they would begin to yell for their sisters and mama. It was the signal for the women to start heating the grease that would fry the fish for supper. If they had enough cornmeal, there would be hush-puppies on the side. As a child, I would get a glimpse of those days when I watched my father cleaning fish for our own family's supper table. As he deftly scraped away the scales and removed the innards, he must have been remembering the many times he did that same thing as a young boy.

Some struggling families received government assistance during those lean Depression years. As my father remembered, Mema Carrie was told they were ineligible because they had a grove. A grove producing grapefruit that nobody had the money to buy. It was a bitter memory.

A widow living with children in the sparsely-developed Florida in the 1930s had to be tough, able to stand up for herself. Carrie was. Circumstances finally allowed the purchase of a car which took her and the kids to town...when there was enough money for gas, that is. The story goes that one day, the family realized that their gas was disappearing. As they sat listening one dark night, they heard stealthy noises in the vicinity of the car. Mema Carrie picked up her rifle, cracked the back door and opened fire. The gas thefts ceased—and some days later, a man showed up in the nearby village with buckshot in his leg.

Her life was so full of losses and hard times that she must have stirred up many pots of grits. But the memories I have of her, as her oldest grandchild, are of a pleasant lady. I remember a self-controlled woman who sang the old hymns of the church as she went about her daily chores. From the songs she sang, I know she was a woman of faith who appreciated the natural world around her. She could grow anything and especially enjoyed working with her rosebushes. When I was four and five years old and my parents were starting the family grove business, I often spent whole days with her. I would stand beside her and watch as she carefully made the cuts in the rose stems, placed the bud inside and wrapped it with cloth. I could walk with her and pick up the avocadoes that had fallen from the tree in the back yard. I could listen to her speak lovingly of that faraway place of her birth called the Eastern Shore.

Only later did I realize what a gift that time was to my life! The atmosphere she created in her home was one of sweet peace and laughter. The Lord lifted her head and she faced each new day armed with resolve. Her attitude was simple: she would do what she had to do. Sick or well, she would deal with it, with God's help and a pot of grits.

Feel the Breeze

How has your family coped with the challenges of life? What stories or memories sustain and inspire you?

CONTRASTS

Grow old along with me...the best is yet to be.
—Robert Burns

EVER SEE YOURSELF AS OTHERS SEE YOU? OR LOOK AT YOURSELF in light of where you are in life?

I'm a person who is perpetually 16 in her head. But these images sometimes come frightfully clear. It happened to me this morning.

Ed and I were strolling down the street in Blowing Rock, North Carolina. It was one of those delightfully misty, cool days that Floridians go to the mountains to enjoy. After a summer of blazing heat, October in Blowing Rock is hard to beat. We had stuffed ourselves with a late breakfast of eggs, grits, sausage and biscuits and headed out to explore the cute little shops along main street.

I saw them about half a block ahead of us. A young couple— they were kids, really—obviously in the grips of young lust. They were standing in the middle of the sidewalk, locked in an embrace, enjoying a passionate kiss. After a moment, they turned and playfully walked ahead of us, arms swinging, faces laughing. But it wasn't the romance that caught our attention. We certainly still have affection, albeit the affection of years and not youth.

What set them apart was their jeans. We had our jeans on, too, but theirs were different. We noticed his first. As he turned to walk ahead of us, it looked like his pants were about to fall off. In the fashion of young men today, the waistband was barely caught by his hips and the legs pooled over his sneakers. Hers, on the other hand, gave new meaning to the term "skin tight." She looked like she had painted them on this morning. Not only were they skin tight at the top, the legs of the pants were molded to her legs all the way down to her shoes. I couldn't imagine how she could stand what had to be their discomfort.

They—the couple and their jeans—were the image of youth.

And walking along behind them, there we were. A mature couple. Ed had his hands in the pockets of his K-Mart special jeans, constructed with room to spare. His leather belt kept things nice and neat, with his shirt tucked in over his tummy. My arm was looped through his, while my other hand slid comfortably into the pocket of my snazzy black jeans. Thank God for that little bit of spandex manufacturers add to women's jeans today. My days of torturing myself for fashion are long over and my body isn't a perfect size anything. Talk about an example of the opposite ends of the love spectrum!

The Bible talks about love—physical love—in some pretty explicit language. "Let him kiss me with the kisses of his mouth— for your love is more delightful than wine," reads Song of Songs 1:2. "My lover is mine and I am his," says Song of Songs 2:16.

Young love and old love. I chuckled as we walked there on the street of Blowing Rock. Ed and I have weathered things that young couple has surely only heard about. They're dreaming dreams, we're seeing visions of eternity. They have desires, we have memories. They're perfect specimens—but we are survivors.

Would I trade places? No. I might enjoy getting back a little of the lust and a lot of the energy.

But not at the price of walking in their shoes…or wearing their jeans.

Feel the Breeze

How do you look at love through the lens of years? What has changed? What has stayed the same?

DANCING THE SKY

He makes the clouds his chariot
and rides on the wings of the wind.
—Psalm 104:3

O I have slipped the surly bonds of earth
And danced the sky on laughter-silvered wings...
Put out my hand and touched the face of God.
—John Gillespie Magee, Jr., *High Flight*

THE GREY SQUIRREL FLUFFED HIS TAIL AND STOOD UP ON HIS hind legs. An acorn was held protectively to his chest. His nose twitched as he eyed me. He's one of my regulars so I know he realized what a strange event he was witnessing.

"Hey, crazy lady," he seemed to be saying, "what in the world has come over *you?*"

What had "come over me" had literally come over me...and the high-pitched whine of the powerful jet engine announced that it was about to come over me again. I looked to the top of the trees to the east of my house. Zipping into view just barely above them, the dark blue supersonic jet whipped overhead. Gold letters clearly visible on the underside of the wings read *U S NAVY.*

The Blue Angels had come to town!

I stood in the middle of my quiet street, waving my flag in greeting. Since our house is directly in the flight path for the runway, every time the blue planes approached from the east they almost brushed the roof of the house. It was thrilling. Sometimes one flew by alone, sometimes two and occasionally four in formation. It was the formation that really brought tears of pride to my eyes.

I'm usually a more reserved person—not someone to weep or celebrate in the street in front of everybody, including the squirrels. But if this combination of awe and patriotism doesn't give a gal permission to act foolish, I don't know what does.

The Blue Angels were the featured performers at the Vero Beach Air Show that year. The first two days in town they rehearsed their well-planned maneuvers over our heads. The show was Saturday and Sunday. I had not planned to actually go to the airport for the show—until they started giving me my personal teaser. Come Saturday, there I was sitting in the hot sun on the tarmac in my lawn chair, bottle of water at the ready. The smell of burgers and hot dogs and sunscreen mixed with the aroma of jet fuel was the special perfume of the day.

And the Blue Angels did not disappoint. Neither did the opening acts, with their women pilots and other participants. What man—and woman!—has accomplished in the air is beyond amazing. Time and again the crowd *oohed* and *aahed*—and sometimes shrieked—as the pilots pushed the machines beyond conceivable limits.

Later that night, as I stared into the dark of my bedroom and pondered the events of the day, I thought about those pilots, especially the pilots of the Navy planes. They would leave the end of the runway and turn the nose straight up…climbing, climbing until they were almost out of sight, just a tiny speck in the sky. It seemed so effortless as the plane gently rolled over and then screamed toward earth. But what do they see? Is their life up there just a blur? Can they actually see those of us who are wildly jumping up and down and waving our flags? Probably not, but they see God's creation in a way we never will.

Those pilots, I like to think, have an appreciation of the vastness of space and time and a perspective of the smallness of man. David said it in Psalm 8: "What is man that you are mindful of him?…O Lord our Lord, how majestic is your name in all the earth."

Sometimes we're reminded of our smallness in ways that make us feel fearful or sad. For me, though, the Blue Angels remind me of man's place in God's universe in a way worthy of celebration.

Amen, David! And thank you, Blue Angels!

Feel the Breeze

God's world has so many "awe-full" sights. When do you look at Creation and get chills?

_____

_____

_____

_____

_____

_____

_____

_____

_____

_____

THANKSGIVING

In everything give thanks;
for this is God's will for you in Christ Jesus.
—1 Thessalonians 5:18

THANKSGIVING DAY, 2001.

My father was dying. In and out of awareness, he had stopped eating weeks before.

We had been sharing the duties of caring for Daddy in his last days. He was at home, in the place he loved, in the recliner he loved to sit in, looking out at the river he loved as well. When he looked out the window next to his chair, he could see across to Memorial Island and the flag. As long as Kennedy Groves was in business, he had made sure a large American flag was raised over it every day, so we knew that the island's flag would please him.

Since our focus was entirely on his care, Thanksgiving was almost lost in the shuffle. Early in the week, my sister-in-law Joy and I brainstormed for a few minutes about what we should do. We knew we would all gather at Mom and Dad's house, as we always had, but who in the world would make the food? None of us were in any shape to create the usual lavish Thanksgiving meal. As we talked, I thought of our cousin. She and her husband own a gourmet grocery store with a wonderful deli. I called her and she took over.

Thanksgiving morning, she and her husband arrived with a turkey dinner and all the trimmings. It was wonderful to see it all—and even more wonderful not to have to cook it.

All my life, Daddy had always said the grace before we ate. He always used the exact same words, short and sweet and to the point. He may not have been very inventive, but it was crucially important to him. Sometimes, he would stop in the middle of his meal and say "Did we say the blessing?" And in spite of all assurances that we had, he would say it again.

Sometimes, when Daddy was distracted, this would happen two to three times during a meal. It got to the point that my brother Kenny and I would look up after the second or third "Amen" and say "Two" or "Three."

That Thanksgiving, Daddy roused when the food came. Holding hands, we all made a circle around his chair. As we stood around him, we said his blessing: "Lord, make us thankful for all of these blessings. We ask it in Jesus's name, Amen."

We went on to fill our plates and enjoy the food. Daddy went back to sleep. He didn't wake up again. He passed peacefully in the early morning hours of that Saturday. Kenny, Mom and I were with him.

It had been the most difficult Thanksgiving I had ever spent. But also a moment touched with grace.

I'm profoundly glad to know that the last thing my father saw was his family gathered around him, saying his blessing.

And as he taught us to be, we were thankful.

Feel the Breeze

When have your family or friends come together for a bittersweet occasion? How did you feel God's grace?

_____

_____

_____

_____

_____

_____

_____

_____

_____

_____

PITCHFORK THEOLOGY

You can't run away from trouble—there ain't no place that far.
—Uncle Remus

If you're going through hell, keep on going.
—Winston Churchill

They reeled and staggered like drunken men;
they were at their wits' end.
Then they cried out to the Lord in their trouble,
and he brought them out of their distress.
He stilled the storm to a whisper;
the waves of the sea were hushed.
—Psalm 107:27-29

I T WASN'T WHAT I WANTED TO BE DOING.

If I had been able to choose, wielding a pitchfork to pick up the mountains of debris the hurricane had left in my yard would have been way down at the bottom of the list.

But hurricanes don't give you choices. As sweat trickled into my eyes and ran in rivers over every part of my aching body, I had lots of time to think. My first thoughts were along the lines of *Rats, how long is this going to take?* After a while, I settled into the realization that it was going to be a lot longer than I wanted and that I'd better get into a different mindset. After that, I began to muse on the question I had heard from so many people in the past few days: *What is God trying to tell us? Why do we have to suffer the wrath and destruction of a hurricane?*

Ed and I had spent the long hours of the storm's fury in the safety of our daughter's new home, miles away from the river's rising waters and their threat to our own home. We were anxious about the house. It had just been renovated, and the roof was the only thing we had not replaced. For all we knew, that roof could have blown away. During the worst hours of screaming wind, I can remember lying in the darkness thinking that we might not even get to live in the house we'd spent so much money and time renovating. Then my thoughts turned to prayers for the safety of people, not things.

Now we were on the other side of the storm. My prayers for safety had been answered, but it was left to us to clean up the mess in our yard. My husband was a man obsessed. He attacked the debris with a fury, chainsaw buzzing as he cut the downed limbs into lengths we could handle. He's a person who wants a mess to be cleared as quickly as possible—but sometimes his idea of "quickly" doesn't feel so possible to the rest of us.

I don't usually share in the yard work. So it took me a minute to find gloves and get into the groove of what he wanted me to do. I found my first experience with a pitchfork to be simple, repetitive—and exhausting. I got into a rhythm after a while, gaining an appreciation for the art of what I was doing. Slide the fork under a pile. Scoop it into the cart. Mash down the stuff in the cart with a satisfying "whump." Fit another pile of stuff in the cart. Slide, lift, whump…slide, lift, whump. Haul the cart to the curb and dump it. Wipe sweaty face with sleeve of tee shirt. Start all over.

Somewhere in those hours, my husband made the comment that the next time we went shopping we should get a new pitchfork. I looked at the one I was using and noticed it for the first time. Its handle was broken off about a quarter of the way from what should have been its top. What remained of it was smooth, attesting to years of rubbing by working hands.

"We've got that one because your daddy gave it to me," Ed explained.

Oh. I looked at the instrument anew. Daddy had been gone almost three years by then, but his influence still threaded its way through our lives every day. Suddenly, the broken handle made sense. Daddy wasn't much on maintenance, but he was thrifty. Just because the handle of the pitchfork had broken was no reason to run and buy something new. As I went back to work, I had a vision of him working in the grove with his pitchfork, his clothes wet with sweat, stopping to wipe his face with a stained handkerchief and keeping on till the job was done. I don't think he ever asked why he had to use a pitchfork. I think he was glad he had a pitchfork to use and a reason to use it.

I got to know that pitchfork pretty well. The mess was so huge it took us days to clean it up. That was when I got around to addressing those bigger questions. Is God angry with us? Have we become too materialistic? Have we taken our eyes off Him? Do we need to be reminded of His sovereignty?

Maybe, I thought, the hurricane came because we need a glimpse of what life is like for others: for the many souls around the world who don't have what we have. Maybe we need to be reminded what it's like to be without electric power, spouts that gush potable water, inside toilets that flush. Maybe we need to remember that air conditioning is a luxury, not a necessity, and only a small percentage of the world's population knows what it's like to have cable television.

Maybe...maybe...maybe...

Maybe it was just our turn.

I didn't have the answers. I only knew that there were many lessons to be learned in a storm. When we stop fretting and fussing and fearing, we can re-focus our eyes on the One who alone has the power to help us make sense of it all. The verses from Psalm 107 that I quoted above describe people in the midst of a storm. Now, I felt their gratitude in a new and deeper way.

Our storm had been stilled. We were safe. It was time for the questions to stop, thanks to be given, and the the mess to be cleaned up.

Maybe, I thought as I worked, privileged middle-aged women just need to learn the lessons that are taught from the business end of a pitchfork.

And instead of "why," perhaps the question is "why not?"

Feel the Breeze

What disasters have blown through your life—natural or otherwise? How did they help you see God in new ways?

Winter

FEET

How beautiful are the feet of them that preach the gospel of peace
and bring glad tidings of good things.
—Romans10:15

FEET. NOT SOMETHING WE THINK ABOUT EVERYDAY, THAT'S
for sure. We use them and go on our merry way. We sometimes
see others who aren't able to use theirs, and it causes us to stop
and be thankful.

A few years ago, my husband and I were living in our home-
town, where much of our family still resides. It was hurricane
season. That year just happened to bring four hurricanes back to
back, all directly affecting Vero Beach, Florida. We had no power
or running water, right in the heat of the summer. We desperately
wanted air conditioning and a shower. My uncle was kind enough
to let us all come and stay on his boat, where a generator provided
all the comforts we used to take for granted at home.

As we were resting that night watching TV, I happened to
look at my uncle's feet. Funny, I thought, they looked just like
my grandfather's feet. My uncle had taken over the family

This essay was written by my daughter, Becky Loar. A piece by her sister, my
other daughter Lyn, appears on page 143. I read the words of my grown-up
girls and I am honored. I'm sure my parents would be, too.

business, and in many ways had stepped into my grandfather's shoes.

As I think of my own feet, they are definitely my father's feet. Wide!

I am thankful to my earthly father for leading me to my Heavenly Father. And I wonder, what would my Heavenly Father's feet look like?

Dusty. Tired. Bloody and nail-scarred.

I'm thankful that I don't have to have nail-pierced, bloody feet, as He took the nails in my place, for me.

Yet I want to inherit my Heavenly Father's feet.

Feet that are kind with steps of purpose. Feet that will lead my children on that path of righteousness and bring encouragement to others.

We are called to walk in the steps of our Heavenly Father. May we seek to fill His shoes in all that we do.

Feel the Breeze

Shoulders capable of bearing burdens, helping hands, discerning eyes: how do your features suggest ways you can be of service in God's kingdom?

THROUGH ANDREW'S EYES

May God, who comes to us in the things of this world
bless your eyes and be in your seeing.
May Christ, who looks upon you with deepest love,
bless your eyes and widen your gaze.
May the Spirit, who perceives what is and what may yet be,
bless your eyes and sharpen your vision.
May the Sacred Three bless your eyes and cause you to see.
—Jan L. Richardson, *In the Sanctuary of Women*

"MIMI, LET'S GO IN THE CHRISTMAS SHOPPE," ANDREW SAID excitedly. "I want you to see something in there. I saw it the last time I was here with Mom and Dad. You'll like it, Mimi! Come on!"

I followed—gimping across the parking lot into the store. It was already packed with brilliant baubles, dazzling decorations and blaring music of the season even though it was just October. I followed my eldest grandson through the maze of the store as he determinedly wound his way to a far back corner. I had no idea what we were there to see, only that my grandson wanted to show me something special.

"There!" He stood before a display of brightly colored small items, each no bigger than three to four inches tall. "Mimi, aren't they neat?"

I looked closer to determine what was so neat about them. And yes, they were quite unique. I was looking at a group of carved wooden objects, each one a different vegetable carved to look like an animal. A cabbage pig, zucchini duck, cucumber frog, banana dog, carrot rabbit, peanut squirrel…you get the idea.

Andrew and I stood for a long time enjoying the little creatures. Andrew is fifteen years old, very bright, and in many wonderful ways a "typical" teenaged boy. He likes girls and loves all things electronic. But he still has an innocence of spirit that sets him apart from others his age. He is enchanted with small things. Items that he can hold in his hands and create a story around are very special to him. How many 15- year-old boys would even notice such small things, let alone remember exactly where they were? How many fewer than that would want to show these small delights to their grandmother?

Because Andrew has such an affinity and appreciation for the itty-bitty pieces of life, I'm learning to see them, too. Isn't it interesting to think that our grandchildren can help us learn to perceive and appreciate more richly and more deeply?

In her book *In the Sanctuary of Women*, Jan Richardson devotes several pages of devotional thoughts to what might be called "deep sight." What do we see and how do we see it? She challenges us "to look at what is around us, to look again, to look more closely, to open ourselves to the God who lives among all this and who invites us to see differently."

Biblical accounts of Jesus's life speak often about healing the blind. As Richardson reminds us, these stories don't apply only to those of us who are literally unsighted. They are about figurative blindness too.

Andrew has a way of seeing life deeply—of not taking sight itself, or the sights of this world, for granted. And because he sees things that others would often overlook, he leads those around him to see them too.

May he always look for the small, the colorful, the interesting things along his way—the details that fill the world with bits of wonder. And may he always remind his Mimi to do the same.

Feel the Breeze

What small, apparently insignificant objects, gestures or moments might you pause and savor— in all their vivid detail—today?

A MOTHER WHO WORKED

She sets about her work vigorously;
her arms are strong for her tasks.
—Proverbs 31:17

But Martha was distracted by all the preparations that had to be
made... "Martha, Martha," the Lord answered... "Mary has chosen
what is better, and it will not be taken away from her."
—Luke 10:40-41

I KNOW WHERE MY MOTHER'S PHYSICAL BODY IS. BUT THE person who spends her days slumped over in a wheelchair in a facility that takes remarkably good care of her is at once my mother, and not my mother. She is but she's not. She barely recognizes me and her memory has lost all the beautiful things of her life.

Since I live in the town where I grew up, I have many friends who passed through our life back then. I have been searching for my mother in their memories, and my own.

"The image I have of your mother is working at the fruit stand," one of them told me. "Most of us girls had never seen a working mom, and she was very unique to me. I wondered how she did it and was a housewife too. She was ahead of her time in that respect, and a role model to some of us."

Kind words from a sweet friend I've known since early childhood. And how those words capture my mother. Mama worked, as her own mother—a remarkable woman who did what she needed to do to survive the poverty of the Depression—had before her.

As I think about my mother's life today, two words come to mind: work ethic. My mother had a work ethic few could match. Anybody wanting to keep up with her had to pick 'em up and lay 'em down. She could walk faster than anybody I've ever known. Most of the time the territory she was covering was from the front to the back or the back to the front of our citrus retail store. She took care of merchandising the front end, stocked with thousands of jars of jelly and cans of orange blossom honey. She was the one that stocked the chocolate fudge alligators and the pecan logs. The items themselves looked festive, but keeping them stocked and shining required constant effort.

And then she went home and cooked supper. Did laundry. Cleaned the house. Raised us kids.

Even in times of leisure—which were rare—Mama was still busy. If nothing else, she was working at the business of play. One thing is certain: in the words of Ecclesiastes, whatever her hand found to do, she did it with all her might.

As I recall how hard she worked, I feel her true presence again.

Yet I also feel a sadness. If I could wish one thing for her, I would wish she could have found some more "Mary" to balance the "Martha" in her life.

You remember the Biblical story of the two. Jesus had come to visit the two sisters. Mary simply celebrated the visit. She was intently focused on every word he had to say, literally sitting at his feet to soak up his presence. Martha went nuts, doing and fixing so everything would be just right for their meal.

Jesus finally had to scold her. "You're worried and upset about many things but only one thing is needed. Mary has chosen what is better and it will not be taken from her."

Yet as a woman who worked myself, I know how hard it is to *stop* working. Once you're in the habit of making sure the shelves are always stocked, the clothes are always washed, the kids are always fed, it's difficult to set that instinctive vigilance aside.

When I visit my mother next, I'm going to do two things.

The first is to thank her for the discipline and work ethic she taught me.

The second will be harder.

I plan to sit with her as a Mary rather than a Martha. I will do my best to turn off the mental checklist of problems to be fixed, both in her room and beyond. I will remind myself that God is with us.

I will simply sit in His presence, and hers.

Feel the Breeze

Has an endless "to do" list denied you time to sit quietly in God's presence? When could you commit some time to being still, letting Him fill your mind?

SING TO THE LORD

I will sing to the Lord as long as I live;
I will sing praise to my God while I have being.
—Psalm 104:33

AS I BACKED OUT OF THE GARAGE, THE RADIO CAME ON AND a beloved familiar voice filled the car. How many mothers, I smiled to myself, get to ride around listening to their daughter's gorgeous voice singing God's praises?

Not many. For me, the CD that I was hearing was the culmination of a long and winding road. We have always had music in our home and our girls were raised with the music of the church ringing in their ears. Being involved in the choirs at our church—at all age levels—was a joyous activity. For three of us, the singing was a happy pastime. For Becky, however, it became her life.

And because it's her life, we share the road with her. It's really a crazy roller coaster ride. We share the highs and lows, the ups and downs, the glowing successes and the moments of sheer misery. All those pretty performance moments are bred out of a myriad of moments of angst and frustration that are not always pretty. Rehearsals are often terrible and the fear of a bad result brings on tears and anger. Singers have bad days and voices don't cooperate. As with every other endeavor in life, you do your preparation and give it your best. And do it and do it and do it.

For a mother, being in the audience for those first big performances is closer to torture than joyful enjoyment. I will always remember a certain morning in Vienna, Austria, when Becky's high school chorus competed against choral groups from around the world. Thanks to their outstanding director, our young people were fine tuned and well prepared. As luck would have it, our group drew the first performance spot, which meant they were in the auditorium ready to sing at 9 a.m. In these competitions, there is no time for every group to perform the totality of every number they have prepared. The judges ask for an excerpt, and you never know which one. On this day, their request was to begin singing at a measure in the middle of an *a capella* piece— right at Becky's solo, which then went into a dramatic few measures that drove the music to its conclusion. Becky had to hit it dead on from the first note or the whole choir would be off. I stood in the back of the auditorium—in those days, it was rare for me to ever sit down during a performance—and hugged my arms across my middle to steady my queasy insides. And I prayed. That clear voice rang through the room exactly on pitch and the competition was on. Our chorus won the entire competition. Celebration!

Becky went on to study classical music, finishing her education with a vocal performance degree. Once she was married and had children, she refocused her attention to the music that was her first love. Classic sacred music, as well as the songs of artists like Sandi Patti and Amy Grant, was always the bedrock of her repertoire. Making a recording was always a dream. The details of creating such a project just never came together until God's intervention put her in contact with one of the leading arrangers and producers of Christian music, Camp Kirkland. So a long path finally led to the beautiful music that filled my car this day.

It is a beginning. Another project is in the works. In the meantime, she continues teaching voice and being a wife and mommy. She does concert work whenever possible. Everything happens in its time.

Becky is living proof of that old joke: How do you get to Carnegie Hall? Practice, practice, practice! It was a happy day when she called me with great excitement in her voice. "Mom! I just came in the stage door at Carnegie Hall and the doorkeeper knew my name!"

I'm often asked, "What should I do to help my talented children develop to their fullest potential?"

The answer is obvious, but not easy. Get the best teacher you can find and seize every opportunity you can to let them perform, exhibit, or create. But keep God's will and their needs as children in balance with those efforts. Time to worship, pray, learn, and simply play are crucial to raising a healthy and happy Christian child, a goal that is just as important as honing talent. It's not always an easy balance to find, as horror stories of destructive "stage door" parents prove.

Better still than the day Becky called me from Carnegie Hall was the Saturday morning some years later when she gathered her family and closest friends for the launch of her CD. She thanked everyone who had supported and encouraged her along the way. And then she sang her hymn arrangement of "The Solid Rock."

On Christ the solid rock I stand;
all other ground is sinking sand...

Amen. Helping my daughter develop and share her talents fully has been wonderful. But watching—hearing—her use them to celebrate God's glory is priceless.

Feel the Breeze

Are there young people whose God-given talents need an encouraging word or a helping hand? Or dreams of your own that you need to pursue?

THE LAST LOOK

Do not let your hearts be troubled. Trust in God; trust also in me.
In my Father's house are many rooms...I am going there
to prepare a place for you.
—John 14:1-2

THEY STOOD IN FRONT OF THE COFFIN, STARING AT THE WOMAN inside. This was the last time they would see her on this earth. I couldn't see their faces from where I sat, but I'm sure there were tears. How could there not be?

The two standing at the coffin were my daughter Lyn and her husband, mourning the loss of his mother. She had been 73, but her death was unexpected—a sudden, heartrending shock.

Ed and I sat far back in the church, waiting for the service to begin. As I looked at them, I was reminded of a time years ago when he and I had stood the same way. Young and stricken, we had stared at his father's face, still not believing this strong man could be gone from our lives so early, at the age of only 49.

Ed's father had so wanted grandchildren. He barely knew Lyn, who was just 11 months old when he died. He would never know her sister, who would come to us two years later. It was one of the saddest times of my life. I would have done anything to help my husband with his grief; I just didn't know how.

Lyn is older than I was then; David's mother was 73. But chronology doesn't really matter. These moments of the last look, the final earthly goodbye, are so wrenching, especially when the passing is sudden and without warning.

Yet again I feel that helplessness in the face of a loved one's grief. But then I remember a favorite hymn. Russell Kelso Carter's timeless words ring so true: "Standing on the promises that cannot fail…" As Lyn and David made their way back to the pew, those promises echoed gently in my mind. John 14:2, with its reassurance that "I go to prepare a place for you." John 14:27, which assures us that "Peace I leave with you, my peace I give you. I do not give to you as the world gives. Do not let your hearts be troubled and do not be afraid."

That day, peace for me was the assurance that my children know the One who *is* peace.

As much as they were hurting on this day, their troubled hearts would heal, and they would find comfort in the days to come…whether or not I could find the words to give it.

Feel the Breeze

What hymn, text or Scripture comforts you in the face of loss, reminding you of God's promises?

EMBARRASSMENT

For I am about to fall, and my pain is ever with me.
—Psalm 38:17

I HAD A BLINDING, POUNDING MIGRAINE HEADACHE.

Headaches had plagued me since I was ten years old. With the stress of college they had grown steadily worse. I knew the drill by this time. The pain started behind the eyes, growing more intense with all my efforts to fight it. I had two choices. I could either take some medicine, turn off the lights, go to bed and scrap all my plans for the evening. Or I could push on and risk nausea and its disgusting result.

I was 21 years old. And a University of Florida coed. And I had a date. Not with just anybody; with my steady boyfriend of over a year. I needed our time together almost as much as I needed breathing. It was Saturday night, doggone it, and our plans called for dinner and a movie. "I have a headache" would sound so false, so phony. I decided to get myself together and go. Maybe I'd feel better after dinner.

I don't know how things are these days, but in the early 1960s the guys on the UF campus could be divided into two camps. There were the slobs and then there were the other guys. The slobs always looked like they just rolled out of bed and fell into the nearest clothes. They were always wrinkled, unshaven and unkempt as they slouched across the campus in their flip-flops.

My fella, on the other hand, was one of the neatniks. He was always buttoned down and tucked in, combed and clean shaven. He strode across campus in his neatly polished shiny brown penny loafers.

That night, he looked as good as ever. And I did feel a bit better for awhile. We ate, we talked, and we went on to the movie.

And then it really got bad. If it had been any other kind of movie, I might have had a chance. Maybe if we had seen a light movie, I could have held my own. One of those foolish things they were putting Elvis into at that time—*Viva Las Vegas* or *Blue Hawaii*, say.

But no. We were intent on taking in the heavy duty intellectual movie of the moment. It was called *The Pawnbroker*, and it was a monstrously intense black-and-white film. I don't remember a whole lot about the story line, except that it had its roots in Nazi Germany. The main character, played by Rod Steiger, spread angst across the screen like black paint from a giant brush. A focus of the story was a spindle—a six-inch nail driven through a crude piece of board—on which the pawnbroker spiked the tickets for the items he received every day. In the scene that climaxed the story, the pawnbroker ran his own hand down that tall nail... slowly. Of course, the camera recorded every gory detail in a ghastly close-up.

As we left the theater, I tried for nonchalance as I gulped air I hoped would beat back the nausea. But I was a goner. The black heat of the pain in my head was winning. I clutched my boyfriend's hand as we walked across the street to his fastidiously detailed Chevrolet Corvair Monza. He reached over and opened the door for me. I leaned over and hurled my dinner all over those shiny brown loafers. As if that wasn't bad enough, some of it bounced from the pavement and splattered on the car.

I should have known better than to go on the date at all. I wanted the ground to swallow me whole. I knew crying would make the pain in my head worse, but I couldn't help it. The nausea and pain took a back seat to mortification on the ride back to the dorm. My fella assured me everything was okay. I didn't believe him. I was convinced that everything would never be okay again.

I was wrong, and he was right.

The hand that wiped my face and dried my tears that night was the same one that brought my coffee to my bedside this morning.

When I read the message of Psalm 34:18—"The Lord is close to the brokenhearted and saves those who are crushed in spirit!"—I sometimes think of that night. God in his goodness was right there helping both of us. That night did as much as anything to make us realize that we belonged together…and has given us decades of laughter, too.

Feel the Breeze

When have you felt God's presence despite, or even because of, moments of embarrassment or shame?

_____

_____

_____

_____

_____

_____

_____

_____

_____

_____

_____

A THIN PLACE

It is crucial that women listen to one another.
—Jan L. Richardson, *In the Sanctuary of Women*

FEW BOOKS THAT I'VE READ IN MY LIFE HAVE IMPACTED MY soul and my thinking as much as Jan L. Richardson's *In the Sanctuary of Women: A Companion for Reflection and Prayer.* Where heaven and earth meet is sometimes described as a "thin place"—a place or moment in time when the barrier between the material and spiritual realms seems so transparent, so gossamer, that the two join. Richardson's book gives me that feeling of connection, reflecting my desire for the presence of God in the midst of the mundane living of everyday things.

I don't know what led me to this book. I was surfing the book sale sites on the Internet and it popped up. The accompanying message was something akin to "you might like this." Thankfully, I took the suggestion…and was reminded of familiar female stories as well as introduced to women from the annals of history that I might not have discovered on my own.

Richardson searches the spirit of Eve and her "original hunger." She shares the mundane yet glorious life of St. Brigid. The Desert Mothers come alive through her telling. Have you ever heard of

Hildegard of Bingen? You will meet her here. And you'll meet Harriet Powers, a slave who left us only a pair of quilts that depict Bible stories, the work of her own hands. Richardson asks, "What does God the creator desire to make known in the world through the work of our own hands?"

I learned a bit about their biographies. But even better, Richardson delved into their prayer lives and their service to God. All of the women in the book are different from each other and from me, but she has gathered us together "in the company of others whose stories both echo and challenge our own."

For example, she tells of a group of nuns in Germany, each of whom created her own prayer book. When the books were found underneath the floor of the convent 500 years later, they had much in common. Yet each was unique and distinctive to the woman who used it. As Richardson affirms, as women we are so much the same, yet also so different.

"It is crucial that women listen to one another," she says, "that we acknowledge both the similarities and differences in the details of our lives..." And so she compiled a book that reflects on women, from Eve down to those of us in the present day, drawing insights and blessings that enlighten and encourage and inform.

My copy is highlighted, has notes in the margins and is visited on a regular basis. I find something new each time I pick it up.

Each devotional essay ends with a poetic Blessing, with words so carefully chosen that each one resonates. I share just one Blessing with you...the one that follows the reading titled *The Gospel of a Woman's Life:*

That you will let yourself be lost
from time to time
in the labyrinth of the Word.
That you may, for a while,
empty yourself of all the words you know.
That Christ the living Word
will find you
and fill you
with his wisdom.
That he will write himself anew
across the pages of your life.
—Jan L. Richardson

I encourage you to explore this wonderful book if you have not encountered it yet. And, if you have books that have been a "thin place" for you, share them—with me and with others.

Feel the Breeze

What books—or works of art, or pieces of music—create a "thin place" for you?

FRIENDS

Give me two months to roam the hills and weep with my friends,
because I will never marry.
—Judges 11:37

JUDGES 11 TELLS THE STORY OF JEPHTHAH, A MIGHTY WARRIOR.
Because of a complex history of wanderings and seizing lands—a
sort of Jewish tale of "gotcha"—Jephthah is called upon to wage
war against the Ammonites. He is a godly man and he asks the
Lord to deliver the Ammonites into his hands. In return, he makes
a promise. *If you will do this, Lord, the first thing that comes out of*
my door when I get home will be offered to you as a burnt
offering.

I'm amazed that anyone would make such a vow. There's no
guarantee that the first thing through the door will be the family
sheep or goat. Sadly for Jephthah, it wasn't. It was his precious
daughter, his only child.

But that's not the part of the story I want to dwell on here.
What's memorable to me is what follows. First, I'm moved that
his daughter is in total agreement that he must keep his vow to
God. What she says to her father next tears my heart.

Do whatever you must to me, she says, *but please give me two months that I can roam the hills weeping with my friends for I will never marry.*

Jephthah's daughter spent her last days weeping, but she did not weep alone.

I very often get teary from a variety of sources—good music, praising the Lord, babies' little toes, great moments in sports. But rarely do I weep, sob, suffer gut-wrenching emotion.

Except for the night I was beyond distressed over my daughter. My fears for her personal and spiritual safety were overwhelming. My friend Judy could tell just by the tone of my voice over the phone that I was at a breaking point. That's what happens after decades of ups and downs, good stuff and rough stuff and *really* rough stuff, giggles and guffaws, sighing and crying. We can enjoy silly, fun things together—texting each other during *Dancing with the Stars* is a new pleasure—but our bond goes much deeper than that. We know each other better than anyone else on earth except maybe our husbands.

In what seemed like mere moments, she was at my door. "Get in the car," she said. She drove to the beach and led me to the steps of the boardwalk. As the waves rolled in and out, she sat with me while I soaked her, myself and the sand with huge tears, weeping like I had never cried before.

I went home drained. But at least I had not wept alone.

Friends are the ones who come in when the whole world has gone out. I've often heard a true friend defined as someone you could call at 3 a.m. My definition is this: a true friend is one who will sit and listen to you weep uncontrollably. A friend who will shed tears with you and, just as important, allow you to shed every one of your own.

Jephthah's daughter had that kind of friends.

I am blessed. I do too.

Feel the Breeze

It's 3 a.m. and all is not well. Who will you call, and how will their support and presence strengthen you?

ON THE ARM OF HIS CHAIR

Draw near to God and he will draw near to you.
—James 4:8

EVERY OUNCE OF MY BEING WAS RIVETED ON THE VIDEO OF The Truth Project. From the depths of his heart, Dr. Dell Tackett shared about our need simply to spend time in the presence of God.

Imagine, he said, what it would be like if we could actually see God—and see how he longs to spend time with us. Picture him with his arms outstretched, beckoning each of us to "Come here...come and sit awhile and talk with me." If we could really get that picture in our minds and hearts, Dr. Tackett said, we would never want to leave that sweet presence of the Lord God.

The image of the outstretched arms of a loving father struck a chord with me. My own father was a loving man with a big lap that was always ready to welcome little ones. But the memory that gives me the best image of this fatherly communion is the time I spent on the arm of the big rocking chair with my maternal grandfather, who we called Papa.

Papa was a peaceful man who loved a rocking chair. He and Mema Jessie always had oversized porch rockers right there in their living room. Everybody knew which chair was which. Those rockers had wide arms, just the right size for a child's bottom. Being pulled up into the curl of Papa's arm, perching on the arm of the chair and sometimes leaning my head on his shoulder, took me to a place of peaceful rest and total safety like I've rarely known since then.

"Get us an apple, hon," he would often say. I would run to the bowl in the kitchen, bring back the fruit and reclaim my spot on his chair. In my absence he would have taken his small knife from his pocket. Carefully, diligently, he would proceed to peel the apple. Starting with the stem end, he would peel around and around until the apple was naked and the peel was a perfect un-broken string. He sliced small pieces of apple meat, one for me and one for him, until our treat was finished. But the ritual didn't stop there. The remains were dropped neatly into the nearby wastebasket. Finally, Papa's knife was wiped clean and returned to his pocket. God was never mentioned while I sat with him, at least not that I remember. Yet His presence was everywhere around us.

We form our ideas about God from the experiences we have on earth—not just the dramatic events but also the mundane moments. The many hours I spent on the arm of Papa's chair did for me exactly what Dr. Tackett spoke about: gave me a palpable, personal sense of God's presence and its sweet safety, peacefulness, and ease.

"Draw near to God," says to my heart. "Come here and sit on the arm of my chair. We'll talk if we want, we'll share an apple, we'll just enjoy being here together."

Feel the Breeze

Do you have an earthly memory or experience that gives you a sense of God's sweet presence? Is it with a person…in nature…something else?

IMPOSSIBLE FEATS OF MOTHERHOOD

She watches over the affairs of her household and does not eat the
bread of idleness. Her children arise and call her blessed...
—Proverbs 31:27-28

MY READING THIS MORNING TOOK ME TO THIS WELL-KNOWN, often-quoted, sweepingly idealistic passage at the end of Proverbs. Every time I read it, I think "How did she do all of that?"

The answer is obvious and amazingly simple: she's a mother.

A godly wife and mother (hopefully I fall into that category, though of course there are some days I doubt it) "is worth far more than rubies." All of the many deeds described in this passage tell us a basic truth: she does whatever is needed to be done for the good of her family. If she is heard muttering under her breath, you can be sure she's likely praying. "Lord, help me. Help me, Lord!"

Every mother has her list of impossible feats. The Proverbs 31 list is truly impressive. I read it with awe but then I think: *Yes, but did she ever drive a fifteen-foot Budget Rental truck from New York to Florida loaded with her daughter's belongings including a big black tuxedo cat named Boy in a carry-cage?*

I won't burden you with the many further details of the odyssey. Just imagine a daughter who needs to be moved, two husbands (mine and hers) who are working and can't help, a truck neither gal quite knows how to drive and that does not have cruise control, a city in which it's impossible to park, a volume of possessions too large to be easily moved, a goodly number of felons who will be happy to divest you of that excess, and an extremely long, boring drive. Oh, and that cat, who doesn't want either to be found or to eat.

Then there are the confusing directions, the leg cramps, and the two zombie-like creatures who finally arrive home.

There are feats of motherhood that play to one's natural gifts and strengths. This wasn't one of them.

But that doesn't matter to a mom.

Seconds after I handed the truck keys to my husband with a plea that he go turn the darn thing back to the rental agency, daughter Becky wrapped me up in a big hug.

"Thanks, Mom."

She didn't have to say anything else. Those are the words a mother lives for. That's how my children rise up and bless me, and yes, it's worth far more than rubies.

Feel the Breeze

What assistance have you offered as a mother or mother figure? Take a moment to celebrate the children you gave it to.

KNOCKING ON THE DOOR

You must try your hardest to get in through the narrow door, for many, I assure you, will try to do so and will not succeed. For once the master of the house has got up and shut the door, you will find yourselves standing outside and knocking at the door crying 'Lord, please open the door for us.'
—Luke 13:24-25 MSG

HE WAS ONE OF THOSE COLLEGE PROFESSORS WHO WAS LEG-endary. Memorable. The kind you talk about with love and respect for the rest of your life.

His name was Buddy Davis. Among other things, he taught reporting, editorial writing and photojournalism. It was my privilege to suffer in his journalism classes at the University of Florida in the early 1960s.

Every student in the journalism degree track from those days remembers Mr. Davis's famous "train wreck" class. The students were in the classroom, which was set up like a newsroom. Mr. Davis was in his office. Acting as the reporter at the scene, he would randomly call in to the waiting student reporters. In a breathless voice, over a really bad phone connection, he would offer "reports," spouting out the facts and then hanging up abruptly as the desperate reporter-in-training cried "What?? Wait!!" It was then up to the student to interpret the reports and craft a story for the next edition of the imaginary newspaper.

At the end of the class, Mr. Davis would appear in the "newsroom," disheveled, dirty and—ostensibly—exhausted.

"We did it!" he would pant. "We covered the story and got the paper out!" His pleasure was infectious. No matter how panicked we had been mere moments before, everyone in that classroom felt a sense of accomplishment.

Mr. Davis loved that kind of teaching. And he was so good at it. In later years, his editorials in *The Gainesville Sun* earned him a Pulitzer Prize. I sent a card of congratulations and received a typical reply—the same sentiment, I'm sure, that he sent to all his students. "Yes, winning the Pulitzer was a highlight of my career," he wrote, "second only to your graduation from the university."

So I have a lot of wonderful memories about Mr. Davis. But the thing I remember best wasn't those moments in class or those great editorials.

It was how he locked the classroom door.

When the bell rang for class to begin, Mr. Davis slammed the door and locked it. You were supposed to be in your seat, ready to go, when the bell rang. Running down the hall wasn't good enough.

The bell rang. Mr. Davis locked the door. And then he stood on the classroom side of it and giggled. No, it was more of a cackle. The more you knocked, the longer you would wait to get in…if, indeed, he let you in at all. I'm sure that in his personal life, he was an understanding fellow. But as a teacher, he had a point to make. I had this experience a couple of times, and I can tell you that it was miserable and embarrassing and something you didn't want to repeat.

Sooner or later, you figured out what to do to avoid it. You realized the importance of advance preparation. If your unfortunate class schedule required you to hoof it from the opposite side of campus in 15 minutes, you figured out the fastest route and didn't tarry. And the next time you had to sign up for one of his classes, you made it your business to build in some extra time beforehand.

Revelation 3:20 says, "Behold, I stand at the door and knock: if any man hear my voice, and open the door, I will come in to him, and will sup with him, and he with me."

Even though my experience with Mr. Davis was decades ago now, every time I hear a Scripture reference like that one, to knocking on the door, I picture myself before Mr. Davis's classroom door, begging for entrance.

Like that door, Heaven's door requires advance preparation. Happily, it doesn't matter if we're later than we should be. To go through Heaven's door, we just need to be on a first name basis with the Doorkeeper. He *wants* to let us in. After all, he knocked on the door of our heart first.

And this time, it's up to us to open it.

It's a profound comfort to know that when I knock on Heaven's door, I won't hear somebody cackling on the other side!

Feel the Breeze

How have you "knocked on the door" in your life? How does that experience illuminate Christ's invitation?

WHEN CHRISTMAS COMES
TO OUR HOUSE

So they came with haste and found Mary and Joseph,
and the baby, who was lying in the manger.
—Luke 2:16

"Maybe Christmas," the Grinch thought,
"doesn't come from a store."
—Dr. Seuss, *The Grinch Who Stole Christmas*

SO WHERE DO YOU THINK CHRISTMAS COMES FROM? IF YOU'RE
like me, you know it comes from your heart, and you do everything you can to create the heart of Christmas in your home and
family every year...especially when there are little ones in the
family.

That's why grandmas buy all that dumb stuff. Stuff that moves
and sings and plays and dings and jingles. Stuff that lights up.
Basically, stuff that needs batteries. Stuff that makes retailers love
us.

I have that stuff. And my grandkids, through the years, have
loved it. Let me be clear about one thing right here: it's not the
stuff that makes the season happy for me. It's the kids' reaction

to the stuff. The Grinch is right. Christmas isn't in the stuff. It's in the eyes of the kids.

Over the years I've collected four of those little plush scenes put out by Hallmark—the ones that have snowmen and chipmunks and Christmas trees. I love it when they wish me a merry Christmas and go rockin' around the Christmas tree. They all have different songs. Of course the kids think it's a riot to get them all going at the same time—though that doesn't amuse their PawPaw.

My most successful Christmas "stuff" purchase ever is a brown fuzzy reindeer in a rocking chair. He has a goofy grin pasted across his face. When you squeeze his paw, he rocks back and forth and plays "Grandma Got Run Over By A Reindeer." Maybe you've seen one of his bazillion brothers. Maybe—God bless your bones—you've even got one of your very own.

My grands absolutely love this guy, who has entertained them for amazingly long stretches of time. In fact, it cracked me up this year when Nathaniel did exactly the same thing his older cousin, Jack, used to do at just about that age. He sat down in his rocking chair in front of the reindeer in his rocking chair and they rocked back and forth in unison to that silly song.

Yes, little ones do indeed get a huge kick out of these toys—so much so that they play them over and over and over again. It's enough to leave you searching your heart for your Christmas spirit!

Luckily, there's a simple way to get it back again.

On the 28th replay or so, I take the little hands and lead them to the living room, away from the lure of the crazy noisemaking stuff. That's when I sit down in front of the nativity scene and talk about Jesus. Tell them why we're having this celebration.

Share with them about the baby in the manger and his mother and his earthly father. Show them the shepherds; talk about the star and the angels that sang on that night.

It's never too early to tell them the baby came from heaven because he loves us and wants us to live with him.

Sure, I love the "stuff" and the kids' reaction to it.

But that moment in front of the nativity scene: *that's* when Christmas comes to my house.

Feel the Breeze

When does the real meaning of Christmas come to your house? With the first Christmas hymn, a child's wonder, some quiet moment special only to you?

AND ALL THE PRETTIES WERE LEFT

Never mind about your belongings,
because the best of all Egypt will be yours.
—Genesis 45:20

I SAT ALONE IN THE HOUSE. SILENCE FILLED THE SPACE ALL around me. My heart broke but I mourned without tears. I had known for years that this house and all that was in it would be mine when she died. She anticipated giving it to me and I looked forward to having it. And now the time had come.

"Thank you," I spoke into the living room air.

The house was far from empty. It was filled with the gatherings of 93 years of life…a life spent in loving a large extended family, doing a lot of hard work, and traveling the world. Empty? Hardly! Every corner was filled with her treasures: Venetian porcelain, dolls, figurines. The curio cabinets displayed the souvenirs she had collected from the far corners of the world. The china cabinet was stacked with dishes of all descriptions plus teapots and teacups she had carefully brought home in her luggage. I knew her drawers and closets were overflowing with lovely clothes, shoes, purses, scarves, jewelry.

Uncle Tom had died more than 20 years before. Since they had no children, he and Clyde had poured their lives into their

nieces and nephews, one of whom was me. The common sentiment among all of us was, "She was like a second mother to me."

And now I sat here, in the house she left to me, with all its
pretty things that she enjoyed so much. It seemed so sad, but life
ends that way for all of us. All the pretties are left behind.

Then I read the line quoted above from the life of Joseph. As
he prepared his long-lost family to leave their homeland and settle
with him in Egypt, he told them to travel light and not be concerned about the belongings they would leave behind. They
would have all the best Egypt had to offer.

The verse helped me put things in perspective.

In her last journey, Clyde traveled light. She left all her pretties
here. The fact is, these figurines and dishes and teacups and pretty
clothes are nothing compared to the glories that surround her in
heaven. She sits in *lux perpetua*...light eternal...and more magnificence than I can ever imagine.

Truly, the best of that *new* home is hers.

Feel the Breeze

What are you keeping and releasing as you walk through this life and God's world?

THE HUSBAND

*Husbands...be considerate as you live with your wives, and treat them
with respect...as heirs with you of the gracious gift of life, so that
nothing will hinder your prayers.*
—1 Peter 3:7

*Don't marry the person you think you can live with; marry only the
individual you think you can't live without.*
—Dr. James C. Dobson

I STARTED THIS BOOK WITH A DEDICATION TO MY HUSBAND.
Ed Holbrook has been by my side since 1963. Yes, he's the neatnik
whose shoes caught the barf the night we saw *The Pawnbroker.*

He is so important in my life that I need to say just a few more
things about him in closing.

The first is that he meant it when he said everything was okay
that night, even though I had just vomited on his shoes. He is
genuinely kind and deeply accepting. The second is that once he
had gotten me back to the dorm that night, he drove straight to
a place with a hose and washed the yuck off his car and his shoes.
Profoundly kind he may be, but he's not one to tolerate a mess.

I should also add that though I never did it again in quite that
spectacular a way, I have made many messes Ed has had to clean

up over the years. I was so amused the other night when Turner Classic Movies ran *The Odd Couple*. There we were, right there on the screen, Felix and Oscar. He's Felix. I'm—sadly—Oscar, Felix's opposite. I am as naturally untidy as Ed is naturally neat. Hopefully, I don't think I've ever told him to leave stuff alone, that I'm not finished dirtying up yet. But I've come close.

Our opposite personalities have created some memorable moments. Especially since our marriage had an added dimension... we worked together. Owned a business together. For 20 years.

My parents had always run the grove together, so I had no qualms about it as Ed and I planned our own business. I had learned that if you wanted to get ahead in life, you worked. And raised your kids in the middle of the business and went home and cooked your meals and washed your dishes and made your beds and all the other activities of life. So in all those years when I was working on the Kennedy Groves catalogs and advertising, I was juggling another life. I spent long hours as Ed's sidekick at the drugstore we ran near the beachfront of our town.

Our clientele was primarily elderly, since we were located in a part of town that was mostly retirees. We filled their prescriptions, gave our best advice, sold them lipsticks and aspirin and everything in between, adding it all to monthly accounts. And we delivered it all to their doorstep if they needed it. All the things you would expect from the neighborhood mom and pop apothecary. We had several good reasons to close our doors after 20 years, but there were a lot of customers saddened when we did it.

It wasn't perfect. No business is. We had our squabbles and disappointments and mess-ups along the way. Hopefully, we kept them to ourselves.

Ed was the kingpin of the store. After all, he was the one with the pharmacy license. The stress on him was intense. Since his name was on the door, everybody with a medical need wanted to talk to him. I thought it would help when we added more phone lines. Alas, it just meant that Ed could now talk to more people at one time. It was a lot of pressure.

Looking back now, I realize that Ed runs our home with the same organizational skills he used to run our business. He's the one who keeps track of the bills and remembers what day is garbage or recycling day. He organizes our kitchen cabinets like he arranged the products on the shelves at the store. He even does dishes and folds laundry.

More than all of those mundane things, the man is a phenomenal caregiver. We have taken care of each other in various health situations from the birth of our first child on, and Ed is far better at it than I am. I've said many times that he should give lessons to husbands who need to know how to take care of their wives. Of course, medicine is his bailiwick. When to take it, how to take it, what to expect when you take it. Beyond that, he has the knack for anticipating my needs and keeping life on an even keel.

As is surely true of every other married couple, all the vows we made at that altar on June 10, 1967, have been tested: better/ worse, richer/poorer, sickness/health. There's no way to know, on that wedding day, how you and your partner are really going to deal with all those situations. Often I've looked back and thought, *Well, it wasn't pretty, but we got through it.* And we learned a lot, about each other and ourselves. I know we came through it all with the help of a loving and gracious God, and that God was there with me when I chose this wonderful man as my life partner.

2013 was our biggest challenge yet. My cancer diagnosis was a real attention-getter. I can't imagine going through chemo without Ed. From the first day after surgery he meticulously cared for my incision and the wretched drains. Throughout the low, low days of chemo and its side effects, he made our home a quiet sanctuary of healing. And when my hair began to sprinkle down on my shoulders, into my plate and onto my pillow, he took me to his kind lady barber. Ed sat and watched while she gave me her best buzz cut. Then I put on a hat and he took me out to lunch!

I am truly blessed.

Feel the Breeze

Who is a person you can't live without? How has
God blessed you in that relationship?

_____

_____

_____

_____

_____

_____

_____

_____

_____

_____

MANGER MEDITATIONS

...And laid him in a manger.
—Luke 2

I CAREFULLY UNWRAPPED THE CHINA MANGER AND SET IT IN place in the center under the peak of the china stable. That anything so fragile has survived with my family for so long is amazing. The tiny figure of a kneeling Mary is in pretty good shape. Joseph has a chip or two. I run my finger around the brown glue necklace adorning the neck of one of the Wise Men. He lost his head many years ago and Mama patched him up. Holding him in my hands today still brings back the sick feeling I had as I watched his head roll off the table and under the chair a long time ago.

My visions of what Christmas means were born in this little scene. I don't know when or where Mama bought it. Maybe somebody gave it to her. But I know it meant a lot to her, because she guarded it so carefully every year when she placed it on the table. She would caution me that it was to look at, not touch, but my hands didn't always get the message. Maybe the shepherds and the sheep should come in from this side, I would think. Maybe the shepherds and Wise Men should mingle together. I really tried to be careful. But somewhere along the way, the sheep got chipped and the cow's tail got shorter.

By the time I was five or six, the story was familiar. Mama had told me about the star and the shepherds and the angels. Mostly she told me that Jesus came into the world because He loves us. It's not a Christmas song, but I remember gazing at the manger scene and singing in my little girl voice. "Jesus loves me, this I know; for the Bible tells me so…"

It may be old, with many of the scars and flaws that life gives us all, but this china manger scene centers my heart on the One whose life we celebrate every year. "Dear Desire of every nation, Joy of every longing heart."

Feel the Breeze

What reminds you of the true meaning of
Christmas?

_____

_____

_____

_____

_____

_____

_____

_____

_____

_____

ACKNOWLEDGMENTS

So many friends for so long have asked, "When are you going to publish a book?"

Along the journey I've taken to that goal, I have learned that writing a book is no easy, do-a-little-bit-here-and-there task. Only the encouragement of friends who believed in me and my vision kept me focused enough to keep working the computer keys, translating thoughts to the page, and polishing pages into this book. Judy Deeson, Thea Hollingsworth, and Meta Keen: just knowing you wanted to read it meant so much to me.

How perfect it has been that "heart sister" Judy Deeson, besides being a great encourager, picked up her camera and produced the pictures that grace this book. Coyla Boob so graciously wrote a lovely Foreword. And to the staff at my church, especially Director of Adult Education Becky Oliver: just know that your supportive spirits are more than appreciated.

It's been said that when the student is ready the teacher appears. I met Suzanne Fox when I took her class on *Jane Eyre*. Once we began to talk, I knew that if my essays ever got published, she would be the one to help me. Thank you, Suzanne, for your hours of editing and organizing, and for being tough enough to keep this wandering writer on task. Most of all, thank you for becoming a caring friend.

ABOUT THE AUTHOR

Sue Holbrook is a fifth generation Floridian, a relative rarity in a state full of recent transplants and part-time "snowbirds." She graduated with her Bachelor of Science in Journalism from the University of Florida and started her career working as a reporter for the *Naples Star*. Her professional experience includes directing the advertising, public relations and catalog production for Kennedy Groves, the citrus business her family founded in Vero Beach, Florida. In addition to her work there, Sue and her husband were owners of an independent pharmacy for twenty years.

Faith has always been a central part of Sue's life. First United Methodist Church in Vero Beach has been her church home for three decades. In addition to being a past leader of the Sarah Fellowship women's circle, she has served on the Board of Trustees, the Worship Committee, Long Range Planning Committee and Church Council as well as singing in the Chancel Choir. Sue was instrumental in organizing the team that has brought speakers such as Liz Curtis Higgs and Babbie Mason for women's events at the church.

As a Lay Speaker in the Florida Conference of the United Methodist Church, Sue fills the pulpit of her church several times a year and speaks regularly to women's groups, including a weekly talk for the Ladies Devotional Lunch at her church.

Married to Ed Holbrook since 1967, Sue has had the pleasure of seeing her family grow to include two feisty and beautiful daughters, two Godly sons-in-law, and four grandkids, who she of course believes are the most delightful grandchildren in history. She is currently working on her next book, which will reflect her recent experience with breast cancer and her mother's Alzheimer's Disease.

Sue is an inspiring, engaging, humorous and uplifting speaker who speaks regularly to church and women's groups. She is available for programs from luncheon talks to all day seminars and retreats, which can be accompanied by music of faith from her daughter, singer Becky Loar.

For more information about Faith Breezes or Sue, or to discuss a speaking opportunity, please visit www.sueholbrook.net.